DISCARD

COUNTERREVOLUTION
AND REVOLT

COUNTERREVOLUTION
AND REVOLT

HERBERT MARCUSE

BEACON PRESS BOSTON

Copyright © 1972 by Herbert Marcuse
Library of Congress catalog card number: 79–179150
International Standard Book Number: 0–8070–1532–6
Beacon Press books are published under the auspices
of the Unitarian Universalist Association
Published simultaneously in Canada by Saunders of Toronto, Ltd.
All rights reserved
Printed in the United States of America
Second printing, November 1972

"Die Liebenden" by Bertolt Brecht is © 1967 by
Suhrkamp Verlag and reprinted from *Gesammelte Werke*
by permission of Suhrkamp Verlag and Stefan Brecht.

To Inge
again
and again

ACKNOWLEDGMENTS

My friends Leo Lowenthal (University of California at Berkeley) and Arno J. Mayer (Princeton University) thoroughly read and commented on the manuscript. Intensive discussions with André Gorz helped me to clarify my views.

I did not show the manuscript to my indispensable friend, Barrington Moore, Jr., as I have always done in the past. He was engaged in writing his own new book. My wish is that his book be widely read. For me, it is a necessary correction of my work.

Much of the material in this book was first submitted in lectures delivered in 1970 at Princeton University and at the New School for Social Research in New York City. I gratefully acknowledge a grant from the Hartford Arts Foundation which allowed me to work out the ideas on art in Chapter 3.

My thanks to Arnold C. Tovell and to Beacon Press for many years of faithful and pleasant cooperation.

CONTENTS

**COUNTERREVOLUTION
AND REVOLT**

The Western world has reached a new stage of development: now, the defense of the capitalist system requires the organization of counterrevolution at home and abroad. In its extreme manifestations, it practices the horrors of the Nazi regime. Wholesale massacres in Indochina, Indonesia, the Congo, Nigeria, Pakistan, and the Sudan are unleashed against everything which is called "communist" or which is in revolt against governments subservient to the imperialist countries. Cruel persecution prevails in the Latin American countries under fascist and military dictatorships. Torture has become a normal instrument of "interrogation" around the world. The agony of religious wars revives at the height of Western civilization, and a constant flow of arms from the rich countries to the poor helps to perpetuate the oppression of national and social liberation. Where the resistance of the poor has succumbed, students lead the fight against the *soldateska* and the police; by the hundreds, students are slaughtered, gassed, bombed, kept in jail. Three hundred of them chased and shot down on the streets of Mexico City opened the festival of the Olympics. In the United States, students are still in the forefront of radical protest: the killings at Jackson State and Kent State testify to their historical role. Black militants pay with their lives: Malcolm X, Martin Luther King, Fred Hampton, George Jackson. The new composition of the Supreme Court institutionalizes the progress of reaction. And the murder of the Kennedys shows that even Liberals are not safe if they appear as too liberal . . .

1

THE LEFT UNDER THE COUNTER-REVOLUTION

The counterrevolution is largely preventive and, in the

Western world, altogether preventive. Here, there is no recent revolution to be undone, and there is none in the offing. And yet, fear of revolution which creates the common interest links the various stages and forms of the counterrevolution. It runs the whole gamut from parliamentary democracy via the police state to open dictatorship. Capitalism reorganizes itself to meet the threat of a revolution which would be the most radical of all historical revolutions. It would be the first truly *world-historical* revolution.

The fall of the capitalist superpower is likely to precipitate the collapse of the military dictatorships in the Third World which depend entirely on this superpower. They would be replaced, not by the rule of a national "liberal" bourgeoisie (which, in most of these countries, accepts neocolonial ties with the foreign power) but by a government of the liberation movements committed to introduce long overdue radical social and economic changes. The Chinese and Cuban revolutions would be able to go their own ways—freed from the suffocating blockade and the equally suffocating necessity of maintaining an ever more costly defensive machine. Could the Soviet world long remain immune, or for any length of time capable of "containing" this revolution?

Moreover, in the capitalist countries themselves, the revolution would be *qualitatively* different from its abortive precursors. This difference would vary in degree, according to the uneven development of capitalism. In its most advanced tendencies, this revolution could break the repressive continuum which today still ties socialist reconstruction competitively to capitalist progress. Without this dreadful competition, socialism could overcome the fetishism of the "productive forces." It could gradually reduce the subordination of man to the instruments of his labor, direct production toward the elimination of alienated labor, while renouncing the wasteful and enslaving conveniences of the capitalist consumer society. No longer condemned to compulsive aggressiveness and repression in the struggle for existence, individuals would be able to create a technical and natural environment which would no longer perpetuate violence, ugliness, ignorance, and brutality.

Behind these familiar traits of a socialism yet to come is the idea of socialism itself as a qualitatively different *totality*. The socialist universe is also a moral and aesthetic universe: dialectical materialism contains idealism as an element of theory and practice. The prevalent material needs and satisfactions are shaped—and controlled—by the requirements of exploitation. Socialism must augment the quantity of goods and services in order to abolish all poverty, but at the same time, socialist production must change the quality of existence—change the needs and satisfactions themselves. Moral, psychological, aesthetic, intellectual faculties, which today, if developed at all, are relegated to a realm of culture separate from and above the material existence, would then become factors in the material production itself.

If this integral idea of socialism is now becoming a guide for theory and practice among the radical Left, it is the historical answer to the actual development of capitalism. The level of productivity which Marx projected for the construction of a socialist society has long since been attained in the technically most advanced capitalist countries, and precisely this achievement (the "consumer society") serves to sustain capitalist production relations, to ensure popular support, and to discredit the rationale of socialism. Certainly, capitalism has not been and never will be able to bring its production relations into harmony with its technical capacity; mechanization which could progressively eliminate human labor power from the process of material production would eventually spell the end of the system.* But capitalism can further raise the productiv-

* Karl Marx, *Grundrisse der Kritik der Politischen Oekonomie* (Berlin: Dietz, 1953), p. 593.

ity of labor by enlarging the dependence of the underlying population. In fact, the equation: technical progress = growing social wealth (the rising GNP!) = extended servitude is the law of capitalist progress. Exploitation proclaims its justification in the constant augmentation of the world of commodities and services—the victims are overhead expenses, accidents on the road to the good life.

No wonder then, that where the capitalist technostructure still preserves a relatively high standard of living and a power structure virtually immune to popular control, the people are apathetic if not thoroughly hostile to socialism. In the United States, where "the people" include the vast majority of the blue collar working class, this hostility is directed against the Old as well as the New Left; in France and Italy, where the Marxist tradition of the labor movement is still alive, the Communist Party and trade unions command the allegiance of the larger part of the working class. Is this due only to the depressed living conditions of this class, or also to the Communist policy, with its democratic-parliamentary minimum program which promises a (relatively) peaceful transition to socialism? In any case, this policy suggests the prospect of considerable improvement for the working classes of their prevailing situation—at the expense of reducing the prospect of liberation. Not only the commitment to the USSR but also the very principles of the sustained minimum-strategy lessen the difference between the established and the new society: socialism no longer appears as the definite negation of capitalism. Quite consistently, this policy rejects—and must reject—the revolutionary strategy of the New Left which is tied to the concept of socialism as the break with the continuum of dependence, the break from the beginning: the emergence of self-determination as a principle of the reconstruction of society. But the radical goals as well as the radical strategy are confined to small minoritarian groups, middle class rather than proletarian in their compositions; while a large part of the working class has become a class of bourgeois society.

To sum up: the highest stage of capitalist development corresponds, in the advanced capitalist countries, to a low of revolutionary potential. This is familiar enough and would not require further discussion were it not for the fact that a very *different* reality lies behind the appearance (which is real enough!). The inner dynamic of capitalism changes, with the changes in its structure, the pattern of revolution: far from reducing, it extends the potential mass base for revolution, and it necessitates the revival of the radical rather than minimum goals of socialism.

An adequate interpretation of the paradoxical relation between the destructive growth of capitalism and the (apparent and actual) decline of the revolutionary potential would require a thorough analysis of the neoimperialist, global reorganization of capitalism. Major contributions to such an analysis have been made.* Here I shall try, on the basis of this material, only to focus the discussion on the prospects for radical change in the United States.

II

The prevalence of a non-revolutionary—nay, antirevolutionary —consciousness among the majority of the working class is

* See, for example, Paul A. Baran and Paul M. Sweezy, *Monopoly Capitalism* (New York: Monthly Review Press, 1966); Joseph M. Gillman, *Prosperity in Crisis* (New York: Marzani and Munsell, 1965); Gabriel Kolko, *Wealth and Power in America* (New York: Praeger, 1962); Harry Magdoff, *The Age of Imperialism* (New York: Monthly Review Press, 1970); G. William Domhoff, *Who Rules America?* (Englewood Cliffs: Prentice-Hall, 1967). "Bourgeois" economists such as A. A. Berle and John Kenneth Galbraith agree to an amazing degree with the Marxists as far as the facts are concerned. For a representative anthology see Maurice Zeitlin, ed., *American Society, Inc.* (Chicago: Markham, 1970).

conspicuous. To be sure, revolutionary consciousness has always expressed itself only in revolutionary situations; the difference is that, now, the condition of the working class in the society at large militates against the development of such a consciousness. The integration of the largest part of the working class into the capitalist society is not a surface phenomenon; it has its roots in the infrastructure itself, in the political economy of monopoly capitalism: benefits accorded to the metropolitan working class thanks to surplus profits, neocolonial exploitation, the military budget, and gigantic government subventions. To say that this class has much more to lose than its chains may be a vulgar statement but it is also correct.

It is easy to brush aside the argument of the tendential integration of the working class into advanced capitalist society by stating that this change only refers to the sphere of consumption and thus does not affect the "structural definition" of the proletariat.* The sphere of consumption is one area of the social existence of man, and as such, determines his consciousness which, in turn, is a factor in shaping his behavior, his attitude at work as well as at leisure. The political potential of rising expectations is well known. To exclude the sphere of consumption in its broader social aspects from the structural analysis offends the principle of dialectical materialism. Still, the integration of organized labor is a surface phenomenon in a different sense: it hides the *dis*integrating, centrifugal tendencies of which it is itself an expression. And these centrifugal tendencies do not operate *outside* the integrated domain; in this very domain the monopolistic economy creates conditions and generates needs which threaten to explode the capitalist framework. Anticipating the subsequent discussion, I

---

* See among many other critics Ernest Mandel, "Workers and Permanent Revolution," in *The Revival of American Socialism*, George Fisher, ed. (New York: Oxford University Press, 1971), pp. 170 ff.

recall the classical statement: it is the overwhelming *wealth* of capitalism which will bring about its collapse. Will the *consumer society* be its last stage, its gravedigger?

There seems to be little evidence for an affirmative answer. At the highest stage of capitalism, the most necessary revolution appears as the most unlikely one. Most necessary because the established system preserves itself only through the global destruction of resources, of nature, of human life, and the *objective* conditions for making an end to it prevail. Those conditions are: a social wealth sufficient to abolish poverty; the technical know-how to develop the available resources systematically toward this goal; a ruling class which wastes, arrests, and annihilates the productive forces; the growth of anticapitalist forces in the Third World which reduce the reservoir of exploitation; and a vast working class which, separated from the control of the means of production, confronts a small, parasitic ruling class. But at the same time the rule of capital, extended into all dimensions of work and leisure, controls the underlying population through the goods and services it delivers and through a political, military, and police apparatus of terrifying efficiency. The objective conditions are not translated into a revolutionary consciousness; the vital need for liberation is repressed and remains without power. The class struggle proceeds in the forms of an "economistic" contest; reforms are not made as steps toward revolution —the subjective factor is lagging behind.

However, it would be wrong to interpret this discrepancy between the necessity and possibility of revolution only in terms of a divergence between the subjective and objective conditions. The former are to a high degree in harmony with the latter: the reformist or conformist consciousness corresponds to the attained stage of capitalism and to its omnipresent power structure—a situation which concentrates the political consciousness and the revolt in nonintegrated minoritarian groups, among labor (in France and Italy especially) as well as the middle classes. It is in the objective conditions themselves where the paradox of the "impossible" revolution finds its solution.

The restabilization of capitalism and neoimperialism, which began after the Second World War, has not yet come to an end—in spite of Indochina, in spite of inflation, the international monetary crisis, and rising unemployment in the United States. The system is still capable of "managing," by virtue of its economic and military power, the aggravating conflicts within and outside its dominion. It is precisely the unprecedented capacity of 20th century capitalism which will generate the revolution of the 20th century—a revolution, however, which will have a base, strategy, and direction quite different from its predecessors, especially the Russian Revolution. Its features were the leadership of an "ideologically conscious avant-garde," the mass party as its "instrument," the basic objective the "struggle for the state power."

It is no accident that this kind of revolution could never take place in the West. Here, the capitalist system has not only attained many of the goals which, in the underdeveloped countries, have been the driving power of the modern revolutions, but capitalism has also succeeded, through the constant development of income, the complexity of the instruments of mediation, the international organization of exploitation, to offer to the majority of the population a possibility of survival, and, frequently, a partial solution of immediate problems.*

* Lucio Magri, "Parlement ou Conseils" (1970), in *Il Manifesto: Analyses et Theses* . . . , Rossana Rossanda, ed. (Paris: Editions du Seuil, 1971), pp. 332 f.

The increasing satisfaction of needs even beyond subsistence needs also changes the features of the revolutionary alternative: it becomes the project of constructing a social order which is capable "not only of producing more and of distributing the product better, but also of producing in a different mode, different goods, and of giving a new form to human relationships." *

The mass base created by the relation between capital and labor in the 18th and 19th centuries no longer exists in the metropoles of monopoly capital (and is gradually being altered in the more backward capitalist countries), and a new base is in the making, an extension and transformation of the historical one by the dynamic of the mode of production.

At the latest stage of economic and political concentration, the particular capitalist enterprises in all sectors of the economy are being subordinated to the requirements of capital as a whole (*Gesamtkapital*). This coordination takes place on two interrelated levels: through the normal economic process under monopolistic competition (growing organic composition of capital; pressure on the rate of profit); and through "state management." ** Consequently, ever more strata of the formerly independent middle classes become the direct servants of capital, occupied in the creation and realization of surplus value while being separated from control of the means of production. The "tertiary sector" (production of services), long since indispensable for the realization and reproduction of capital, recruits a huge army of salaried employees. At the same time, the increasingly technological character of material production draws the functional intelligentsia into this process.

* *Ibid.*

** See Seymour Melman, *Pentagon Capitalism* (New York: McGraw-Hill, 1970). However, the term "state management" exaggerates the independence of the state from capital.

The base of exploitation is thus enlarged beyond the factories and shops, and far beyond the blue collar working class.*

Communist strategy has long since acknowledged the decisive changes in the composition of the working class. The following statement is taken from the discussion of the theses for the XIXth Congress of the French Communist Party: ". . . the Communist Party has never confused membership in the working class with manual labor. . . . With actual progress in technology and the growth in the number of non-manual workers, it becomes in fact more difficult to separate manual and intellectual labor although the capitalist mode of production tries to maintain this separation." The statement goes on to say that Marx's concept of the *"travailleur collectif"* is not identical with that of the traditional (wage earning) laboring class: "the *'travailleur collectif'* includes salaried employees who are not laborers, such as researchers, engineers, cadres, et cetera." Today's working class is greatly enlarged: it is composed "not only of the proletarians in agriculture, in the factories, mines,

* The discussion on the "new working class" was sparked by Serge Mallet's *La Nouvelle classe ouvrière* (1963). For more recent literature see J. M. Budish, *The Changing Structure of the Working Class* (New York: International Publishers, 1964); Stanley Aronowitz, "Does the United States Have a New Working Class?" in *The Revival of American Socialism, loc. cit.*, pp. 188 ff.; and André Gorz, "Technique, Techniciens et Lutte des Classes," in *Les Temps Modernes,* August–September 1971, pp. 141 ff. Especially important is Gorz's distinction between the technical-scientific workers who participate in the control of the production process and are actually part of management, and those who are subjected to this hierarchy. See also Herbert Gintis, "The New Working Class and Revolutionary Youth," in *Socialist Revolution,* San Francisco, May–June 1970.

The literature on the New Left and the present phase of capitalism can already fill a library. I like to mention only one—in my view the most articulate, honest, critical, and charming one, written by two young activists: *A Disrupted History: The New Left and the New Capitalism,* by Greg Calvert and Carol Neiman (New York: Random House, 1971).

construction yards who form the core of this class, but also of the sum-total of those workers who intervene directly in the preparation and functioning of the material production." In this transformation of the working class, not only new strata of salaried employees are "integrated" into this class, but also "occupations which were not part of the sector of material production assume a productive character." *

> [Today,] the power of monopoly [capital] becomes articulate no longer primarily in the work relationship [*Arbeitsverhältnis*] but *outside* it, on the market, and in all realms of political and social life. . . . Monopoly capital finds its victims not only among those dependent on it, in such a way that each of us, at some time or other, is caught in the net of capitalist relationships—while it is not excluded that those [victims] who are immediately dependent on it can sometimes be "lesser victims," sometimes even beneficiaries and potential allies.**

The extended scope of exploitation, and the need to integrate into it additional populations at home and abroad, makes for the dominant tendency of monopoly capitalism: to organize the *entire* society in its interest and image.

The directing and organizing power of *Gesamtkapital* confronts the productive power of the *Gesamtarbeiter*† (collective labor force): each individual becomes a mere fragment or

---

* *France Nouvelle.* Hebdomadaire Central du Parti Communiste Français, January 28, 1970.

** Lelio Basso, *Zur Theorie des politischen Konflikts* (Frankfurt: Suhrkamp, 1969), pp. 10, 13 f. (my translation and italics); written 1962.

† See Karl Marx, *Capital,* ch. XVI, second paragraph (New York: Modern Library).

atom in the coordinated mass of the population which, separated from control of the means of production, creates the
global surplus value. Within this mass, the intelligentsia plays
a vital role not only in the process of material production, but
also in the ever more scientific manipulation and regimentation
of consumption and "productive" behavior.

The process of capital-realization draws ever larger strata
of the population into its orbit—it extends beyond the blue collar working class. Marx projected the structural changes which
enlarge the base of exploitation to include previously "unproductive" work and services:

No longer the individual laborer but rather the
socially combined labor power becomes the actual
agent of the collective work process. The various competing labor powers which constitute the productive
machine as a whole participate in very different ways
in the immediate production of commodities (here
rather products). One individual works with his hands,
another with his head, one as manager, engineer, tech-
nologist, et cetera, the other as overseer, a third as
direct manual laborer or mere helper. Thus more and
more functions of labor power are being subsumed
under the immediate concept of productive labor and
the workers under the concept of productive workers.
They are directly exploited by capital. . . . [The combined activity of the collective laborer results] immediately in a collective product which is at the same
time a sum-total of commodities, and it is a matter of
indifference whether the function of the individual
worker, who is only a member of this collective laborer,
is more remote or close to immediate manual labor.
. . . The activity of this combined labor power is its
immediate productive consumption by capital—self-

realization of capital, immediate creation of surplus value. . . .*

Thus, in the internal dynamic of advanced capitalism, "the concept of productive labor is necessarily enlarged," and with it the concept of the productive worker,** of the working class itself. The change is not merely quantitative: it affects the entire universe of capitalism.

The enlarged universe of exploitation is a totality of machines—human, economic, political, military, educational. It is controlled by a hierarchy of ever more specialized "professional" managers, politicians, generals, devoted to maintaining and enlarging their respective dominion, still competing on a global scale, but all operating in the overriding interest of the capital of the nation as a whole—the nation *as* capital, imperialist capital. True, this imperialism is different from its predecessors: more is at stake than immediate and particular economic requirements. If the security of the nation now demands military, economic, and "technical" intervention, where indigenous ruling groups are not doing the job of liquidating popular liberation movements, it is because the system is no longer capable of reproducing itself by virtue of its own economic mechanisms. This task is to be performed by a state which is faced, in the international arena, with a militant opposition "from below" that, in turn, sparks the opposition in the metropoles. And when today, the deadly play of power politics leads to an effective cooperation and an effective division of spheres of influence between the state-socialist and state-capitalist orbit, this diplomacy envisages the common threat

* Karl Marx, *Resultate des unmittelbaren Produktionsprozesses* (earlier version of a 6th chapter of *Capital*) (Frankfurt: Neue Kritik, 1969), pp. 65 f.
** *Capital,* vol. I, ch. XVI, second paragraph. See also *Theorieen über den Mehrwert,* Karl Kautsky, ed. (Stuttgart: Dietz, 1905), vol. I, pp. 324 f.

from below. However, "below" are not only the wretched of
the earth but also the more educated and privileged human objects of control and repression.

At the base of the pyramid atomization prevails. It con-
verts the *entire* individual—body and mind—into an instrument, or even part of an instrument: active or passive, productive or receptive, in working time and free time, he
serves the system. The technical division of labor divides the
human being itself into partial operations and functions, coordinated by the coordinators of the capitalist process. This technostructure of exploitation organizes a vast network of human
instruments which produce and sustain a rich society. For unless he belongs to the ruthlessly suppressed minorities, the individual also benefits from this richness.

Capital now produces, for the majority of the population
in the metropoles, not so much material privation as steered
satisfaction of material needs,* while making the entire human
being—intelligence and senses—into an object of administration, geared to produce and reproduce not only the goals but
also the values and promises of the system, its ideological
heaven. Behind the technological veil, behind the political veil
of democracy, appears the reality, the universal servitude, the
loss of human dignity in a prefabricated freedom of choice.
And the power structure is no longer "sublimated" in the style
of a liberalistic culture, no longer even hypocritical (thus re-
taining at least the "formalities," the shell of dignity), but brutal, throwing off all pretensions of truth and justice.

---

* This change is indicated by the growth in "discretionary income,"
that is, income not required for the satisfaction of basic needs (*Fortune*
magazine, December 1967, estimated this part as one third of all personal
income). See David Gilbert's paper "Consumption: Domestic Imperialism"; prepared as a talk for the Wisconsin Draft Resistance Union Insti-
tute. At the same time, poverty in the United States is rising, reversing,
in 1970, a ten-year trend (Bureau of the Census, reported in the *New
York Times,* May 8, 1971).

True and false, good and bad, openly become categories of the political economy; they define the market value of men and things. The commodity form becomes universal, while at the same time, with the disappearance of free competition, the "inherent" quality of the merchandise ceases to be a decisive factor in its marketability. A President is sold like an automobile, and it seems hopelessly old-fashioned to judge his political statements in terms of their truth or falsehood—what validates them is their vote-keeping or vote-getting quality. To be sure, the President must be able to perform the function for which he is bought: he must be able to assure business as usual. In the same way, the quality of an automobile is determined (and limited) by the margin of profit. The automobile, too, must perform the function for which it is bought, but this "technical" quality is "overlaid" with the qualities required by the sales policy (excessive power, debilitating comfort, shiny but bad material, et cetera).

As the commodity form becomes universal and integrates branches of the material and "higher" culture which previously retained a relative independence, it reveals the essential contradiction of capitalism in its most extreme concentration: capital versus the mass of the working population as a whole.

Within this dependent mass, the hierarchy of positions in the process of production makes for persistent class conflicts— conflicts of immediate interests, for example, between the highly paid technicians, experts, and all sorts of specialists on one side, and on the other, the worker who suffers from this application of technology; between organized labor and the subproletariat of national and racial minorities. The "unproductive" intelligentsia enjoys a greater freedom of movement than the productive laborer. And yet, the separation from control over the means of production defines the common *objective* condition of the wage and salary earners: the condition of exploitation—they reproduce capital. The extension of exploitation to a larger part of the population, accompanied by a high standard of living, is the reality behind the façade of the *consumer society;* this reality is the unifying force which integrates, behind the back of the individuals, the widely different and conflicting classes of the underlying population.

III

This unifying force remains a force of disintegration. The total organization of society under monopoly capital and the growing wealth created by this organization can neither undo nor arrest the dynamic of its growth: capitalism cannot satisfy the needs which it creates. The rising standard of living itself expresses this dynamic: it enforced the constant creation of needs that could be satisfied on the market; it is now fostering *transcending* needs which cannot be satisfied without abolishing the capitalist mode of production. It is still true that capitalism grows through growing *impoverishment,* and that impoverishment will be a basic factor of revolution—although in new historical forms.

In Marxian theory, originally, impoverishment meant privation, unsatisfied vital needs, first of all material needs. When this concept no longer described the condition of the working classes in the advanced industrial countries, it was reinterpreted in terms of *relative* deprivation: relative to the available social wealth, cultural impoverishment. However, this reinterpretation suggests a fallacious continuity in the transition to socialism, namely, the amelioration of life within the existing universe of needs. But what is at stake in the socialist revolution is not merely the extension of satisfaction within the existing universe of needs, nor the shift of satisfaction from one (lower) level to a higher one, but the rupture with this universe, the *qualitative leap.* The revolution involves a radical transformation of the needs and aspirations themselves, cultural as well as material; of consciousness and sensibility; of the work process as well as leisure.* This transformation appears in the fight against the fragmentation of work, the necessity and productivity of stupid performances and stupid merchandise, against the acquisitive bourgeois individual, against servitude in the guise of technology, deprivation in the guise of the good life, against pollution as a way of life. Moral and aesthetic needs become basic, vital needs and drive toward new relationships between the sexes, between the generations, between men and women and nature. Freedom is understood as rooted in the fulfillment of these needs, which are sensuous, ethical, and rational in one.

If the New Left emphasizes the struggle for the restoration of nature, for public parks and beaches, for spaces of tranquillity and beauty; if it demands a new sexual morality, the liberation of women, then it fights against material conditions imposed by the capitalist system and reproducing this system. For the repression of aesthetic and moral needs is a vehicle of domination (see Chapters 2 and 3).

Marx saw in the development and spread of vital "superfluous" needs beyond the basic needs the level of progress where capitalism would be ripe for its end:

> The great historic role of capital is the creation of surplus labor, labor which is superfluous from the standpoint of mere use value, mere subsistence. The historic role of capital is fulfilled as soon as (on the one hand) the level of needs has been developed to the degree where surplus labor over and above work for the necessities has itself become a universal need generated by the individual needs themselves, and (on the other hand) when the strict discipline of capital

* See the platform of the group *Il Manifesto*, especially theses 73, 74, and 79, in *Politics and Society*, vol. I, no. 4; August 1971.

has schooled successive generations in industriousness and this quality has become the general property of the new generation. . . .*

The universal need for work other than and above the necessities is here stipulated as developing out of the individual needs —only under such conditions would the individuals themselves determine the objects, priorities, and direction of their work. At the most advanced stage of capitalism, when work for the necessities is technically reducible to a minimum, the universal need for surplus work would mark the rupture, the qualitative leap. The historical locus of the revolution is that stage of development where the satisfaction of basic needs creates needs which transcend the state capitalist and state socialist society.

In the growth of these needs are the radically new impulses of revolution. The insistence on them in no way indicates a weakening or even abandonment of the primary demand of all revolution, namely, the satisfaction of material needs for all. But it does express the awareness that, from the beginning, the satisfaction of vital material needs must, in the revolution, proceed under the horizon of *self-determination*— of men and women who assert their freedom, their humanity, in the satisfaction of their vital material needs. The human being is and remains an animal, but an animal which fulfills and preserves his or her animal-being by making it part of him- or her-*self*, his or her freedom as a Subject.

The centrifugal forces which appear in the emergence of transcending needs operate behind the back of the capitalist managers, and they are generated by the mode of production itself. The growing productivity of labor, accompanied by a

---

* Karl Marx, *Grundrisse der Kritik der politischen Oekonomie, loc. cit.*, p. 231. See Martin Nicolaus' comments on this passage in *New Left Review*, no. 48, 1968. The passage is also quoted in Calvert and Neiman, *loc. cit.*, p. 103. I have made slight changes in the translation.

declining use of human labor power employed in the production of commodities, necessitates the internal expansion of the market, the counterpart to external imperialism. The established mode of production can only sustain itself by constantly augmenting the mass of luxury goods and services *beyond* the satisfaction of vital material needs (the fulfillment of these needs requiring an ever smaller quantity of labor time), which means augmenting the consumer population (mass of purchasing power) capable of buying these goods.* The misery of unfulfilled vital needs is abolished for the majority of the population; outright poverty is "contained" among a minority (though a growing one) of the population. Technical progress and the vast output of "luxuries" create and re-create, alongside the world of alienated labor (in the daily publicity and conspicuous exhibition of the commodity wealth), the images of a world of ease, enjoyment, fulfillment, and comfort which no longer appears as the exclusive privilege of an elite but rather within the reaches of the masses. The technical achievements of capitalism break into the world of frustration, unhappiness, repression. Capitalism has opened a new dimension, which is at one and the same time the living space of capitalism and its negation. The production of goods and services on an enlarged scale reduces the basis for further capitalist development.

The development of the "tertiary sector," that of "services," henceforth takes place at an accelerated

---

* Michael Tanzer, *The Sick Society* (New York: Holt, Rinehart and Winston, 1971), quotes the "chairman of one of the country's largest corporations, Allied Stores" as follows: "Basic utility cannot be the foundation of a prosperous apparel industry. . . . We must accelerate obsolescence. . . . It is our job to make women unhappy with what they have. . . . We must make them so unhappy that their husbands can find no happiness or peace in their excessive savings" (pp. 155 f.). The policy here applied to the apparel industry governs, *mutatis mutandis,* large sectors of the economy as a whole, including the war industries.

rhythm. It absorbs growing demands and calls for ever increasing unproductive investments. The growth of this sector creates a disequilibrium in the balance of forces which up to now have entirely turned on the multiplication of goods and on the profitability of production.

It is not a paradox if the producer begins to recede more and more before the consumer, if the will to produce weakens before the impatience of a consumption for which the acquisition of things produced is less important than the enjoyment of things living. . . .

The revolt of the young generation against the consumer society is nothing else than an intellectual manifestation of the will to go beyond the industrial era, the search for a new profile of society which is placed somehow beyond a society of producers.*

To be sure, "enjoyment of things living" presupposes their production—though not entirely! Many of them are already there; they just have to be redistributed. And the things needed for the satisfaction of material wants for all could be produced with a minimum of alienated labor. But the creation of adequate surplus value necessitates not only the intensification of labor but also enlarged investments in waste and profitable services (publicity, entertainment, organized travel) while neglecting and even reducing nonprofitable public services (transportation, education, welfare). Even so, monopoly capitalism is threatened with a saturation of the investment and commodity market. Competitive consumption must constantly be augmented—which means that the high standard of living perpetuates life in ever more senseless and dehumanizing forms, while the poor remain poor, and the number of the victims of the *prosperitas Americana* is growing.

* Jacques Rozner, quoted in *Le Monde*, June 23, 1970.

It seems that this contradiction between that which is and that which is possible and ought to be, penetrates, in very concrete forms, the mind of the dependent population. The awareness of the irrationality of the whole adversely affects the performance of the system. The fetishism of the commodity world is wearing thin: people see the power structure behind the alleged technocracy and its blessings. Outside the small radical minorities, this awareness is still unpolitical, spontaneous; repressed time and again; "ideological"—but it also finds expression at the very base of society. In spreading wildcat strikes, in the militant strategy of factory occupations, in the attitude and demands of young workers, the protest reveals a rebellion against the *whole* of the working conditions imposed, against the *whole* performance to which one is condemned.

> The younger generation, which has already shaken the campuses, is showing signs of restlessness in the plants of industrial America. Many young workers are calling for immediate changes in working conditions and are rejecting the disciplines of factory work that older workers have accepted as routine. Not only are they talking back to their foremen, but they are also raising their voices in the union halls complaining that their union leaders are not moving fast enough. [The younger workers] are better educated and want treatment as equals from the bosses on the plant floor. They are not as afraid of losing their job as the older men and often challenge the foreman's orders.*

One knows one can live otherwise. Acts of individual and group sabotage are frequent. Absenteeism has reached tremen-

* From a report by Agis Salpukas in the *New York Times,* June 1, 1970. For more recent documentation on the growing scope of workers' complaints, see *Time* magazine, November 9, 1970, pp. 68 ff., and *Newsweek,* May 17, 1971, pp. 80 ff.

dous proportions! * Among salaried employees (sales personnel, office workers, et cetera), indifference—even hostility—toward the job are conspicuous: one doesn't care. "Efficiency" is outdated; the thing goes on anyway. Previously, during the period of free competition, the functioning of capitalism depended largely on the responsible identification of the person with his job, his function—an identification forced upon the worker, but an integral part of good business for the bourgeois: bankruptcy threatened the indifferent and the inefficient. Today, when a whole sector of the economy (agriculture) and a large sector of industry depend on government subsidies, bankruptcy is no longer a threat.

For the great majority of the population, mind and body have always been experienced as instruments of "socially necessary," painful performances. In fact, the entire culture, and particularly the introjected religion and morality, insisted on this necessity—part of human fate, a precondition for reward and enjoyment. The rationality of the repression organized in the capitalist mode of production was obvious: it served the conquest of scarcity and the mastery of nature; it became a driving force of technical progress, a productive force. Today, the opposite is the case: this repression is losing its rationality. "Inner-worldly asceticism" goes badly with the consumer society; it is replaced by Keynesianism with a vengeance.

With a vengeance: the very policy which was to assure the further growth of capitalism did so while aggravating its contradictions. In the United States, which is still the protector

---

* "Even in a time of recession, the absentee rate has remained disturbingly high. . . . Ford Motor Company reports that absenteeism has more than doubled in the past ten years and in 1970 averaged 5.3 percent. . . . One auto company offered green stamps for regular attendance. (It didn't work.) And on top of absenteeism, many young workers in auto plants simply walk out." Newsweek, May 17, 1971, p. 80.

of "capital as a whole," this protection necessitated the construction of a military machine which has become a leader in the control of capital.* The global expansion is driven to its limits: in Latin America, in Asia, in Europe, the American hegemony is effectively challenged.**

And in the consumer society, internal counterpart to neoimperialism, the trend is likewise reversed: real wages are declining, inflation and unemployment continue, and the international monetary crisis indicates the weakening of the economic base of the empire. A potential mass base of social change finds its diffuse, prepolitical expression in the work attitudes and protests which threaten to undermine the operational requirements and values of capitalism. Can one not make a living without that stupid, exhausting, endless labor—living with less waste, fewer gadgets and plastic but with more time and more freedom? This century-old question, which has always been denied by the facts of life imposed by the lords of the earth, is no longer an abstract, emotional, unrealistic question. Today, it assumes dangerously concrete, realistic, subversive forms.

Does the consumer society really appear as the last stage of capitalism? "Consumer society" is a misnomer of the first order, for rarely has a society so systematically been organized in the interests which control *production*. The consumer society

---

* "As of June 1969, property owned directly by the Department of Defense amounted to $202 billion. This included land, buildings, production equipment, offices, communication facilities, airports, and the value of purchased military equipment. By 1969, the Department of Defense owned twenty-nine million acres of land. The scope of resources controlled by the Department of Defense is further revealed in the size of the contracts awarded in a given fiscal year. Thus, for fiscal year 1967, $44.6 billion in contracts were awarded by the Department of Defense," Seymour Melman, *Pentagon Capitalism, loc. cit.,* p. 72.

** Ernest Mandel, *La Réponse socialiste au défi américain* (Paris: Maspero, 1969); Claude Julien, *L'Empire américain* (Paris: Grasset, 1968); Harry Magdoff, *loc. cit.*

is the form in which monopoly state capitalism reproduces itself at its most advanced stage. And it is at this stage that repression is reorganized: the "bourgeois-democratic" phase of capitalism terminates in the new counterrevolutionary phase.

The Nixon Administration has strengthened the counterrevolutionary organization of society in all directions. The forces of law and order have been made a force above the law. The normal equipment of the police in many cities resembles that of the S.S.—the brutality of its actions is familiar. The full weight of suppression falls on the two centers of the radical opposition: the colleges and the black and brown militants: activity on the campuses is stifled; the Black Panther party has been systematically chased down before it disintegrated in internal conflicts. A vast army of undercover agents is spread over the entire country and through all branches of society. Congress has been emasculated (or rather, has emasculated itself) before the executive power which, in turn, depends on its vast military establishment.

This is *not* a *fascist* regime by any means. The courts still uphold the freedom of the press; "underground" papers are still being sold openly, and the media leave room for continual and strong criticism of the government and its policies. To be sure, freedom of expression hardly exists for the blacks, and is effectively limited even for the whites. But civil rights are still there, and their existence is not disproved by the (correct) argument that the system can still "afford" this kind of protest. Decisive is rather whether the present phase of the (preventive) counterrevolution (its democratic-constitutional phase) does not prepare the soil for a subsequent fascist phase.

There is little need to stress the facts that in the United States the situation is different from Weimar Germany, that there is no strong Communist Party, that there are no paramilitary mass organizations, that there is no total economic crisis, no lack of "living space," no charismatic leaders, that the Constitution and government set up in its name are well functioning, and so on. History does not repeat itself exactly, and a higher stage of capitalist development in the United States would call for a higher stage of fascism. This country possesses economic and technical resources for a totalitarian organization immeasurably greater than Hitler Germany ever had. The Administration may be forced, under the threefold impact of the setbacks in its imperialist expansion, the internal economic difficulties, and the pervasive discontent among the population, to set in motion a far more brutal and comprehensive machinery of control.

I have stressed the unpolitical, diffuse, unorganized character of this discontent. The potential mass base for social change may well become the mass base for fascism: "we may well be the first people to go Fascist by the democratic vote." * The relation between liberal democracy and fascism has found its shortest and most striking formulation in the phrase: "liberal democracy is the face of the propertied classes when they are not afraid, fascism when they are afraid." ** The intensified repression and the new economic policy of state-capitalist controls seem to indicate that, at least in the United States, the ruling class is getting afraid. And among the people at large, a configuration of political and psychological conditions point to the existence of a proto-fascist syndrome. A few examples:

—Just as the labor vote made up a significant part of the vote for George Wallace in the last Presidential elections, so it did in the recent election of the rightist Mayor of Philadelphia, who characterized himself as the toughest cop in the nation. —The prevalence of accumulated violence among the population exploded, in a terrifying way, in the almost religious identification with a convicted multiple war criminal, who was

* William L. Shirer, in *Los Angeles Times*, March 13, 1970.
** Leo Guiliani, in *Le Monde*, July 23, 1971.

hailed as another Christ to be crucified. The outcry was that the war criminal should be honored rather than punished, and by a margin of a hundred to one, letters, telegrams, telephone calls challenged the sentence.*

—I quote the following true horror story on the reaction after the killing of four students at Kent State College in May 1970:

> But no case of parental rejection equals that of a family living in a small town near the Kentucky border with three good-looking, well-behaved, moderate sons at the university. Without any record of participation in protest, the boys found themselves inadvertently involved at the vortex: the middle son ended up standing beside one of the students who was shot (at a great distance from the firing); the youngest was arrested for trespass and his picture appeared in the hometown paper, to the embarrassment of his family. When the family spoke to one of our researchers, the conversation was so startling that more than usual care was taken to get it exactly as delivered.

> *Mother*: Anyone who appears on the streets of a city like Kent with long hair, dirty clothes or barefooted deserves to be shot.
> *Researcher*: Have I your permission to quote that?
> *Mother*: You sure do. It would have been better if the Guard had shot the whole lot of them that morning.
> *Researcher*: But you had three sons there.
> *Mother*: If they didn't do what the Guards told them, they should have been mowed down.

* Richard Hammer, *The Court Martial of Lt. Calley* (New York: Coward, McCann and Geoghegan, 1971), pp. 373 ff. See also my article in the *New York Times,* May 13, 1971.

Professor of Psychology (listening in): Is long hair a justification for shooting someone?
Mother: Yes. We have got to clean up this nation. And we'll start with the long-hairs.
Professor: Would you permit one of your sons to be shot simply because he went barefooted?
Mother: Yes.
Professor: Where do you get such ideas?
Mother: I teach at the local high school.
Professor: You mean you are teaching your students such things?
Mother: Yes. I teach them the truth. That the lazy, the dirty, the ones you see walking the streets and doing nothing ought all to be shot.*

—The concerted attack on education other than "professional" and "hard"-scientific is no longer confined to the normal repression via the budget. Thus the Chancellor of the California State Colleges wants systematic restrictions on the humanities and social sciences, where traditionally non-conformist education has found a niche.

> a lot of students are coming to college who aren't sure why they are there . . . they have gone almost reflexively into the humanities and social sciences without specific occupational goals.**

Once upon a time, it was the proclaimed principle of great bourgeois philosophy that the youth "ought to be educated not for the present but for a better future condition of the human race, that is, for the idea of humanity." † Now the Council for

---

* James A. Michener, *Kent State: What Happened and Why* (Greenwich, Conn.: Fawcett Publications; Random House, 1971), pp. 409 f.
** *Los Angeles Times*, November 17, 1971.
† Kant, *Vorlesungen über Pädagogik, Werke*, Ernst Cassirer, ed. (Berlin: Bruno Cassirer, 1922), vol. 8, pp. 464 ff.

Higher Education is called upon to study the "detailed needs" of the established society so that the colleges know "what kinds of graduate students to produce." *

The monopoly capitalist management of the population, the inflated economy, the "defense" policy of kill and overkill, the training for genocide, the normalization of war crimes, the brutal treatment of the vast prison population have built up a frightening reservoir of violence in everyday life. Whole sections of the big cities have been abandoned to crime, and crime is still a favorite entertainment of the mass media. Where this violence is still latent, verbal, or expressed only in minor acts (such as roughing up of demonstrators), it is primarily directed against powerless but conspicuous minorities who appear as disturbing aliens to the established system, who look different, speak and behave differently, and who are doing things (or are suspected of doing things) which those who accept the social order cannot afford to do. Such targets are black and brown people, hippies, radical intellectuals. The whole complex of aggression and targets indicates a proto-fascist potential *par excellence*.**

The only counterforce is the development of an effectively organized radical Left, assuming the vast task of *political education,* dispelling the false and mutilated consciousness of the people so that they themselves experience their condition, and its abolition, as vital need, and apprehend the ways and means of their liberation.

To be sure, fascism will not save capitalism: it is itself the terroristic organization of the capitalist contradictions. But

* *Los Angeles Times,* November 17, 1971.
** See Leo Lowenthal and Norbert Guterman, *Prophets of Deceit: A Study of the Techniques of the American Agitator, 1949* (Palo Alto: Pacific Books, 1970). T. W. Adorno, Else Frenkel-Brunswik, and others, *The Authoritarian Personality* (New York: Harper and Brothers, 1950).

once fascism is installed, it may well destroy any revolutionary potential for an indefinite time.

A Marxian analysis cannot seek comfort "in the long run." In this "long run," the system will indeed collapse, but Marxian theory cannot prophesy which form of society (if any) will replace it. Within the framework of the objective conditions, the alternatives (fascism or socialism) depend on the intelligence and the will, the consciousness and the sensibility, of human beings. It depends on their still-existing *freedom*. The notion of a protracted period of barbarism as against the socialist alternative—barbarism based on the technical and scientific achievements of civilization—is central to Marxian theory. At present, the initiative and the power are with the counterrevolution, which may well culminate in such a barbarian civilization.

IV

It is on the soil of the counterrevolution that the New Left in the United States (only in the United States?) has its base of operations. It seems to be exceedingly weak, especially among the working class. The radicals are confronted with violent hostility on the part of the people, and they appear as easy targets of prosecution and persecution. But this low of the revolutionary potential at the height of capitalist development is deceptive: the deception disappears if we understand that, at this stage, a new pattern of disintegration and revolution emerges, corresponding to, and engendered by, the new phase of capitalism: monopoly-state capitalism. And understanding this, in turn, calls not for the revision but for the restoration of Marxian theory: its emancipation from its own fetishism and ritualization, from the petrified rhetoric which arrests its dialectical development. The false consciousness is rampant on the New as well as Old Left.

In the preceding section, I sketched the tendencies which make for an enlarged and changing potential mass base and changing "motives" of revolution. They result from the mode of production itself which enlarges (and modifies) the base of exploitation while creating needs which the established mode of production cannot satisfy. The needs are still those for a better life, "rising expectations," but for a life no longer defined by full-time dehumanizing labor—for a life in self-determination. The goal necessitates, on the basis of a socialist mode of production, a total reconstruction of the technical and natural environment.

With this historical shift, capitalism denies its legitimation to rule any longer the life of men and women, to shape nature and society in its own image. Breaking the oppressive rule of material production now shifts the focus from the material to the intellectual sectors of production, from alienated labor to creative work. Or rather, material production, increasingly subjected to technological organization, becomes susceptible to humanization. The weight of dead labor on living labor is reducible through removing progressively living labor from the mechanized and fragmented work process where it is still held by the requirements of capitalist production. The transfer of living labor to "supervisory" functions would open the possibility of changing the direction and goals of material production itself. Human labor, instead of being a commodity producing commodities in accordance with the law of value, could produce for human needs in accordance with the law of freedom —the needs of a liberated human existence; an alternative appears which would involve the subversion of the material *and* intellectual culture. The consumer society raises the specter not only of an economic but also of a cultural revolution: a new civilization where culture is no longer a privileged branch in the social division of labor but instead a culture which shapes society in its entirety, in all its branches, including those of material production, and which radically changes prevalent values and aspirations.

This change is foreshadowed, in an ideological form, by the counterimages and countervalues with which the New Left contradicts the image of the capitalist universe. The exhibition of a noncompetitive behavior, the rejection of brutal "virility," the debunking of the capitalist productivity of work, the affirmation of the sensibility, sensuality of the body, the ecological protest, the contempt for the false heroism in outer space and colonial wars, the Women's Liberation Movement (where it does not envisage the liberated woman merely as having an equal share in the repressive features of male prerogatives), the rejection of the anti-erotic, puritan cult of plastic beauty and cleanliness—all these tendencies contribute to the weakening of the Performance Principle. They articulate the deep malaise prevalent among the people at large.

But precisely these countervalues, this counterbehavior, isolate, in open hostility, the radical movement from "the people." Such isolation has twofold roots: (1) socialist, Marxist theory and practice have no soil, no "sufficient reason," among the large majority of the working population, and consequently, (2) the radical difference between a free society and the existing one remains obscured—as do the very real possibilities of establishing a free society. Liberation thus appears as a threat: it becomes taboo. And the taboo is violated by the political as well as the hippie sector of the New Left. There is an internal connection between the two sectors (apart from all organizational and personal links)—the libertarian features reflect moral and aesthetic qualities of socialism which have been minimized in the development of Marxian theory itself (see Chapter II below). They "anticipate" on an individual and small group level the extreme "utopian" aspects of socialism. Within the existing society, they appear as the "privilege" of outsiders—unproductive and counterproductive (which indeed they are and ought to be in terms of capitalist productivity).

In the political sector, the New Left assumes an apparently elitarian character by virtue of its intellectual content: the concern of "intellectuals" rather than "workers." The predominance of intellectuals (and anti-intellectual intellectuals) in the movement is indeed obvious. It may well be expressive of the growing use of intellectuals of all sorts in the infrastructure as well as in the ideological sector of the economic and political process. Moreover, to the degree to which liberation presupposes the development of a radically different consciousness (a veritable *counter*-consciousness) capable of breaking through the fetishism of the consumer society, it presupposes a knowledge and sensibility which the established order, through its class system of education, *blocks* for the majority of the people. At the present stage, the New Left is necessarily and essentially an *intellectual* movement, and the *anti*-intellectualism practiced in its own ranks is indeed a service to the Establishment.

The isolation of the New Left is thus well founded: far from testifying to the movement's lack of social roots, this isolation corresponds to the actual historical situation; it projects indeed the "definite negation" of the *entire culture* of monopoly capitalism at its most advanced stage. This isolation reflects the unprecedented, "unorthodox" qualities of the revolution, the radical contradiction to the established culture—including the culture of the working class! It is precisely in its extreme intellectual, moral, and "physiological" exigencies that the possibilities—nay, necessities—of the revolution find their most complete and realistic expression. It is the *qualitative* change only which *is* change, and the new *quality* of life which alone can terminate the long series of exploitative societies. These extreme aspects, precisely because of their radically new quality, appear easily as the ideological preoccupation of more or less affluent intellectuals.

Allergic to its factual separation from the masses, not ready to admit that it is expressive of the social structure of advanced capitalism and that its separate character can be overcome only in the long struggle to change this structure, the movement displays inferiority complexes, defeatism, or apathy. This attitude fosters the depolitization and privatization of the hippie sector, to which the political sector opposes its political puritanism in theory and practice.

v

Marxian theory remains the guide of practice, even in a non-revolutionary situation. But here another weakness of the New Left appears: the distortion and falsification of Marxian theory through its *ritualization.* Clearly, the concepts used to analyze 19th and early 20th century capitalism cannot simply be applied to its present stage: being historical concepts, they carry in themselves historical indices, and the structure they analyze is a historical structure. To be sure, capitalism is capitalism in all its phases, and its organization of the mode of production underlies its entire development. However, the capacities of the mode of production also develop, and these changes affect the base and the superstructure. To isolate the identical capitalist base from the other sectors of society leaves Marxian theory at its very foundation with an unhistorical, undialectical abstraction. The changes occur within the capitalist framework; they are internal, gradual, quantitative, but they will lead to the point of the "qualitative rupture," to a prerevolutionary situation. Not to confront the Marxian concepts with the development of capitalism and not to draw the consequences from this confrontation for the political practice leads to a mechanistic repetition of a "basic vocabulary," a petrification of Marxian theory into a rhetoric with hardly any relation to reality. It further fortifies the alienation of the New Left; it severely impairs the communication of its message.

The petrification of Marxian theory violates the very principle which the New Left proclaims: the *unity of theory and practice*. A theory which has not caught up with the practice of capitalism cannot possibly guide the practice aiming at the abolition of capitalism. The reduction of Marxian theory to solid "structures" divorces the theory from reality and gives it an abstract, remote, "scientific" character which facilitates its dogmatic ritualization. In a sense, all theory is abstract: its conceptual dissociation from the given reality is a precondition for understanding, *and changing* reality. Theory is furthermore necessarily abstract by virtue of the fact that it comprehends a *totality* of conditions and tendencies, in Marxian theory; a historical totality. Thus, it can never decide on a *particular* practice—for example, whether or not certain buildings should be occupied or attacked—but it can (and ought to) evaluate the *prospects* of particular actions within the given totality, namely, whether a situation prevails where such occupations and attacks are indicated. The unity of theory and practice is never immediate. The given social reality, not yet mastered by the forces of change, demands the adaptation of strategy to the objective conditions—prerequisite for changing the latter. A non-revolutionary situation is essentially different from a pre- or revolutionary situation. Only a theoretical analysis can define and distinguish the prevailing situation and its potential. The given reality is there, in its own right and power—the soil on which theory develops, and yet the object, "the other of theory" which, in the process of change, continues to determine theory.

The New Left has played a decisive part in sparking the process of change. In the United States, the activation of the black and brown minorities, the popular opposition which has revealed the war crime policy in Indochina, the conflict between the powerful media and the government—these achievements are due largely to the militants of the Left, especially the students. In France and Italy, the radicalization of the economistic trade union demands and of the entire strategy of the Left (the revival of the workers' councils) presents a threat to the powerful hold of the reformist Communist apparatus—in spite of the reversal after May 1968. In these countries, too, the petrification of Marxian theory has been countered by an analysis grounded in the transformation of capitalism and of the potential base of revolution. In the United States, the economic and political conditions call for a still more radical reexamination; it is only in its beginnings.* Pending its further development, the following sections, which try to evaluate the situation of the New Left in the United States, must be highly tentative and fragmentary.

VI

The present situation of the New Left is essentially different from the period during which the radical opposition took shape and had its first nationwide effects (the militant civil rights movement, war resistance, activism in the colleges and univer-

* In France, especially André Gorz and Roger Garaudy; in Italy the group Il Manifesto. For the United States, see the *Monthly Review, Socialist Revolution, Radical America,* some of the publications of the Radical Education Project; and the anthology *The Revival of American Socialism, loc. cit.; The New Left: A Documentary History,* Massimo Teodori, ed. (New York: Bobbs-Merrill, 1969), especially the Second Part. The classical documentation of the primary impulses motivating the New Left still is the *Journal de la Commune Etudiante, Novembre 1967–Juin 1968: Textes de Documents,* Alain Schnapp and Pierre Vidal-Naquet, eds. (Paris: Editions du Seuil, 1968; abridged American edition, *The French Student Uprising, November 1967–June 1968,* Boston: Beacon Press, 1971).

sities, the political Hippie Movement). About ten years ago, the transcending goals, too, became articulate: the new morality, the emancipation of sensibility, the demand for "freedom now," the cultural revolution. The Establishment was not prepared. The strategy then could be massive, open, and largely offensive: mass demonstrations, occupation of buildings, unity of action, juncture with the black militants. The period came to an end when the impact of the New Left became apparent. The withdrawal of President Johnson, the battle at the Democratic Convention in Chicago, and the intensified war in Indochina mark the beginning of the new phase. Not the working class but the universities and ghettos presented the first real threat to the system from within. The Establishment had a keener insight into the seriousness of the threat than the New Left itself. Now the system is prepared—to such an extent that the very survival of the radical movement as a political force is in question. How is the movement reacting to these new conditions?

It appears to be weakened to a dangerous degree. This is primarily due to the legal and extra-legal aggressive repression on the part of the power structure—a concentration of brutal force against which the Left has no adequate defense. This mobilization of power accentuates the internal weaknesses within the New Left, above all: (1) ideological conflicts within the militant opposition and (2) the lack of organization.

The Left has always been divided: this is natural, because, while the predominant interest in private property and in the preservation of its institutions easily unites the defenders of the status quo, no such tangible common goal unites those who aim at abolishing the status quo. They work under an open horizon of several alternatives and goals, strategy and tactics.

But division has not always prevented or even delayed revolution; *vide* the struggle between the Mensheviks and Bolsheviks. Perhaps it is only in such struggles that the "correct" strategy can be tested in practice. However, the situation is different where and when the movement has not yet taken root in a popular base and, above all, when, because of its numerical weakness, it is subjected to easy and effective persecution; in other words, where and when a revolutionary strategy is not on the agenda, but only the preparation of the soil for such a strategy. Such a situation calls for the "suspension" of premature (or obsolete) ideological conflicts in favor of the more urgent task of building up numerical strength. In radical strategy, too, the turn into quality presupposes quantitative growth.

In this context, the problem of communication becomes acute. The more the integral, "utopian" goals of socialism appear as concrete historical goals, the more are they estranged from the established universe of discourse. The "people" speak a language which is all but closed to the concepts and propositions of Marxian theory. Their aversion to its foreign words, "big words," et cetera, not only is the result of their education but also expresses the extent of their commitment to the Establishment and, consequently, to the language of the Establishment. To break the hold of this language means breaking the "false consciousness": becoming conscious of the need for liberation and of the ways to approach this goal. Marxian theory and practice had succeeded in developing the political consciousness of the labor movement when, under the twofold impact of the defeat of the European revolutions of 1918 and the capitalist stabilization, the reversal occurred: confronted with effective trade unionism and effective capitalism, the revolutionary theory assumed an abstract character—the concern of small minorities. It has assumed this character to an even higher degree where no strong Marxist tradition exists. As we have noted, the gap between theory and reality has been enlarged by the widespread reduction of Marx's dialectical concepts to a "basic" vocabulary. The dialectical concepts comprehend reality in the process of change, and it is this process which constitutes the definition of the concept itself. Thus, the transformation of classical imperialism into neoimperialism redefines the classical concept while demonstrating how the new forms derive from the preceding ones. Similarly with "proletariat," "exploitation," "impoverishment." Bombarding the people with these terms without translating them into the actual situation does not communicate Marxian theory. At best, these words become identification labels for in-groups (Progressive Labor, Trotskyists, and so on); otherwise, they function as mere clichés—that is, they don't function at all. Their use as instant stimuli in a canned vocabulary kills their truth. The Marxian concepts define the essence behind the reality: their meaning emerges in the analysis of the "appearance," and the "appearance" of capitalism today is very different from its 19th century stage.

The petrification (*Verdinglichung*) of concepts falsifies the analysis of the class structure of monopoly capitalism. The radical ideology often succumbs to *a fetishism of labor*—a new aspect of the fetishism of commodities (after all, labor power *is* a commodity). Of the three qualities which, in Marxian theory, make the working class the potentially revolutionary subject ([1] it alone can stop the process of production, [2] it is the majority of the population, and [3] its very existence is the negation of being human) of these three qualities, only the first still applies to that part of the American working class which could reasonably be called the contemporary successor of the proletariat: blue collar labor. But the Marxian conception defines the *unity* of the three qualities; the proletariat, constituting the majority of the population, is revolutionary by virtue of its needs, the satisfaction of which is beyond the reaches of capitalist capabilities. In other words, the working class is the potential subject of revolution not merely because it is the class exploited in the capitalist mode of production, but because the needs and aspiration of this class demand the abolition of this mode of production. It follows that, if the working class is no longer this "absolute negation" of the existing society, if it has become a class *in* this society, sharing its needs and aspirations, then the transfer of power to the working class alone (no matter in what form) does not assure the transition to socialism as a *qualitatively* different society. The working class itself must change if it is to become the power that effects this transition.*

If the needs created but not satisfiable by monopoly capital would assume a subversive force and become the soil for the development of political consciousness among the working population, it would not be (this is decisive!) the resurgence of *proletarian* class consciousness; it would not set off a laboring class against all other sectors of the working population, not "wage labor" versus capital, but rather all dependent classes against capital. By the same token, this new consciousness would militate against the framework of trade union policy: it would envisage the end of the established mode of production in its entirety. This is the dynamic of monopoly capitalism: the subjection of the entire population to the rule of capital and its state corresponds to the universal need for its abolition. If this development modifies the original concept of class, if it obscures the sharp contrast between the blue collar laboring class and other sectors of the working population, then it is due to changes in the *reality* of capitalism which have to be conceptualized in the *theory* of capitalism.

True, these are mere tendencies. They meet with inten-

---

* Rosa Luxemburg knew that a radical transformation of the working class was a condition of revolutionary strategy: the working class will acquire the "freely assumed self-discipline of Social Democracy, not as a result of the discipline imposed on it by the capitalist state, but by extirpating, to the last root, its old habits of obedience and servility" (German text in Rosa Luxemburg, *Politische Schriften,* O. Flechtheim, ed. (Frankfurt: Europäische Verlagsanstalt, 1968), vol. III, p. 91. English text as quoted in Calvert and Neiman, *loc. cit.,* p. 151).

sified resistance on the part of the power structure, and they have not yet reduced the gap between the working class and the New Left, especially the radical intelligentsia. It does the latter no good to minimize the hostility of the workers: this hostility is rational and well founded. And yet, the juncture between the two forces is a precondition for change: trade union consciousness must become political consciousness, socialist consciousness. This will not be achieved by "going to the workers," joining their picket lines, espousing their "causes," et cetera. The juncture can only come about in the process of social change in which the two groups act each *from its own base* and in terms of its own consciousness, grievances, and goals. This is, for example, the strategy of the *Sinistra Proletaria* in Italy: "students and intellectuals who previously worked within the base groups in the factories, now no longer agitate in or in front of the factories. There, the militant political propaganda is made by the workers themselves, chiefly young workers, while the students support the workers by supplying material for agitation, research in the various parts of the city, et cetera." * Similarly in France, the group *Base-Ouvrière* at the Renault-Flins factory is organized in an *équipe extérieure* and an *équipe interne*, the former mainly consisting of "intellectuals," the latter (much smaller) of workers in the factory. The internal group is still too weak to "impose its rhythm and direction on the whole Base-Ouvrière." ** Such (temporary) division of functions, which avoids patronizing and the automatic negative reaction, could promote unity to the degree to which the different specific interests of each group, experienced and articulated in its own terms and situation (in the factory, shop, office, neighborhood), find their common ground and common strategy.

* *Zeitdienst,* Zurich, September 11, 1970.
** From a text submitted to the Renault workers by the group Base-Ouvrière, in *Les Temps Modernes,* August–September 1971.

This is very different from the "development of class consciousness from without"; the minoritarian groups of today on which the task of organization will fall will be very different from the *Leninist avant-garde*. The latter assumed the leadership, in theory and practice, of a working class in which it was rooted and which lived with the immediate experience of poverty and oppression—to such an extent that a lost war sufficed to organize it for revolutionary action. And these masses were the human basis for the material reproduction of society. In the imperialist metropoles of today, this situation does not prevail.

Moreover, the Leninist avant-garde was the correlate of a mass *party*, existent or in the making. This was its rationale—otherwise it would have been Blanquism pure and simple. Today, where the Communist parties still are mass parties in opposition, they adhere to a "minimum program" of parliamentary strategy. In their practice (though by no means in their official ideology), they recognize the political weakness and the non-revolutionary attitude of the majority of the working class under advanced capitalism*—an evaluation far more accurate than that of some of the radical groupings on the Left. However, these Communist parties are *not* the Social Democracy of the recent past, and not of the present—in spite of their reformist strategy. For Social Democracy still persists as a working class organization, and the Communist parties and unions are still the only *mass* organizations on the Left of Social Democracy. By virtue of this constellation, they are still a *potentially* revolutionary force.

For the United States (and perhaps not only for the

* Thus the French Communist Party has denounced as "anarchissantes" such rather traditional strategies of the Marxist labor movement as the "unlimited" strike and mobilization of spontaneity. "Spontaneity does not exist" declares a pamphlet distributed by the Communist-controlled CGT after the "leftist" attempt to prolong and extend the strike at the Renault works in Mans in May 1971 (*Le Monde*, July 22, 1971).

United States), the question must be raised whether, under the conditions of monopoly-state capitalism, the highly centralized and hierarchically structured revolutionary mass party is not historically outdated. It belonged to a past stage of capitalist development: to a still liberal phase. Then, these parties operated within a still functioning parliamentary framework, even where they boycotted elections. But when the parliament has become a vehicle of counterrevolution, they lose the political space of operation—all radical opposition becomes extra-parliamentary opposition.

VII

Here may well be the turning point in the strategy of the Left. The sweeping concentration of power and control in the nationwide political and military Establishment necessitates the shift to decentralized forms of organization, less susceptible to destruction by the engines of repression, and more expressive of the divergent and dispersed nuclei of disintegration. Monopoly capitalism has given a new concrete sense to the "revolution from below": subversive grass roots. The technical and economic integration of the system is so dense that its disruption at one key place can easily lead to a serious dysfunctioning of the whole. This holds true for the local centers not only of production and distribution, but also of education, information, and transportation. Under these circumstances, the process of internal disintegration may well assume a largely decentralized, diffuse, largely "spontaneous" character, occurring at several places simultaneously or by "contagion." However, such points of local dysfunctioning and disruption can become nuclei of social change only if they are given political direction and organization. At this stage, the primary autonomy of the local bases will appear as decisive for securing the support of the working population on the spot and for preparing the new cadres in reorganizing production, distribution, transportation, and education.

I have referred to the notion, today widespread among radical groups of the New Left, that "seizure of power" in the sense of a direct assault on the centers of political control (the state), backed and carried out by mass action under the leadership of centralized mass parties—that such strategy is not, and cannot be, on the agenda in the advanced capitalist countries. The main reasons are: (1) the concentration of overwhelming military and police power in the hands of an effectively functioning government and (2) the prevalence of a reformist consciousness among the working classes. Is there a historical alternative?

We recall the pattern of the bourgeois revolution: the attainment of economic power by the bourgeoisie within a feudal society preceded the seizure of political power. To be sure, this pattern cannot simply be passed along to the socialist revolution; but the question arises: are there any indications that the working class might attain economic though not political power within the capitalist system, and prior to a revolution? This would be the case if the workers would take control in the factories and shops, and redirect and reorganize production. But precisely this would be the revolution, and would entail political power. Is a gradual change in economic power (turning quantitative into qualitative change through radicalization of workers' demands and successes) conceivable within capitalism?

Prevailing trends in this direction are highly ambivalent. They may lead to qualitative change; they may lead to further integration of the working class. The integrating trend is suggested by some efforts, on the part of management, to reduce the fragmentation and atomization of work at the conveyor belt and to give the individual worker responsibility and control over a larger unit of the product. According to a report* on such innovations introduced by several electronic factories in the United States, the result was a considerable improvement in the quality of the product and a more positive attitude of the worker toward his job and to the enterprise.

Is it likely that this trend would radicalize the initiative of the workers to the point where their control over their product, over their individual jobs, would be tantamount to the end of the capitalist mode of production itself? Or could the trend be contained without substantially altering the hierarchy in the factory? To drive workers' control beyond the limits of capitalist toleration presupposes the development of a radical political consciousness among the members of the working class; otherwise, workers' control would still be immanent to the established system, its rationalization. Revolutionary workers' control would presuppose the primacy of the political over the economic and technical factors. If this political radicalization to the Left occurs, the system would be weakened and eventually disrupted in the de-centralized, de-bureaucratized way also indicated by the general condition of monopoly capitalism: uneven development: workers' control in individual factories or groups of factories—"nests" of postcapitalist (socialist) units in the still capitalist society (similar to the urban centers of bourgeois power within the feudal society).

Such a development would recapture a seminal achievement of the revolutionary tradition, namely, the "councils" ("soviets," *Räte*) as organizations of self-determination, self-government (or rather preparation for self-government) in local popular assemblies. Their revival is indicated not only by the historical obsolescence of bureaucratic mass parties but also by the necessity to find, as their historical heirs, new ade-

* *Der Spiegel* (Hamburg, Germany), October 4, 1971.

quate sources of initiative, organization, and leadership. The historical heir of the authoritarian mass party (or rather, its self-perpetuating leadership) is not anarchy but a self-imposed discipline and authority—an authority which can only emerge in the struggle itself, recognized by those who wage the struggle. However, the theory and strategy of the councils, too, must not succumb to the fetishism of "below." The *immediate* expression of the opinion and will of the workers, farmers, neighbors—in brief, of the people—is not, per se, progressive and a force of social change: it may be the opposite. The councils will be organs of revolution only to the degree to which they represent the people *in revolt*. They are not just there, ready to be elected in the factories, offices, neighborhoods— their emergence presupposes a new consciousness: the breaking of the hold of the Establishment over the work and leisure of the people.

Direct democracy, the subjection of all delegation of authority to effective control "from below," is an essential demand of Leftist strategy. The demand is necessarily ambivalent. To take an example from the student movement: effective student participation in the administration of the university. In political terms, this demand presupposes that the majority of the student body is more progressive than the faculty and the administration. If the contrary is the case, the change would turn against the Left. The argument is correct but does not imply the conclusion that the demand be dropped. For under given conditions (which are long-range conditions, rooted in the prevailing social tendencies), student control would have a greater chance to introduce badly needed reforms than the present hierarchy, and Leftist strategy must be oriented on these conditions.

This kind of critical evaluation also applies to the much larger question of workers' control. I have just stressed its ambivalence. Workers' control may lead to an alleviation of the burden of work, to its more effective organization, to the development of workers' initiative. But at the same time, these changes may well benefit the capitalist enterprise. Nevertheless, the demand has correctly become central in radical strategy. For such a control would in the long run loosen the link between the work process and the process of the realization of capital; it would eliminate the need for the production of waste and planned obsolescence; it would give technology a chance to shake off the restrictions and distortions to which it is now subjected.

The ambivalence of the "below" also characterizes the Leftist slogan "power to the people." The "people" meant here are not those who today sustain the bourgeois democracy: the voters, the taxpayers, the large number of those who express their opinion in the letters to the editor which are deemed fit to print. These people, though by no means sovereign in any sense, exercise considerable power already, as the constituencies of the rulers, as a derivative power, dependent on the rulers. "Power to the people" does not mean the (anything but "silent") majority of the population as it exists today; it means a minority—the victims of this majority, those who perhaps don't even vote, don't pay taxes because they have nothing to be taxed, those in the prisons and jails, those who do not write letters to the editor which get printed. However, the ambivalence of the slogan expresses the truth that "the people," the majority of the people are *de facto, distinct from,* and *apart from* their government, that self-government of the people is still to be fought for. It means that this goal *pre*supposes a radical change in the needs and consciousness of the people. The people who have the power to liberate themselves would not be the same people, the same human beings, who today reproduce the status quo—even if they are the same individuals.

While it is true that the people must liberate themselves from their servitude, it is also true that they must first free themselves from what has been made of them in the society in which they live. This primary liberation cannot be "spontaneous" because such spontaneity would only express the values and goals derived from the established system. Self-liberation is self-education but as such it *pre*supposes education by others. In a society where the unequal access to knowledge and information is part of the social structure, the distinction and the antagonism between the educators and those to be educated are inevitable. Those who are educated have a commitment to use their knowledge to help men and women realize and enjoy their truly human capabilities. All authentic education is political education, and in a class society, political education is unthinkable without leadership, educated and tested in the theory and practice of radical opposition. The function of this leadership is to "translate" spontaneous protest into organized action which has the chance to develop and to transcend immediate needs and aspirations toward the radical reconstruction of society: transformation of immediate into organized spontaneity.

Spontaneity does not contradict authority: inasmuch as revolutionary practice is the explosion of *vital needs* (which, as we have seen, do not have to be needs for the material necessities of life), it is rooted in spontaneity—but this spontaneity can be *deceptive*: it can be the result of the introjection of social needs required by the established order but militating against the liberation of the human being. This is today the case to an unprecedented extent. The intensive indoctrination and management of the people call for an intensive countereducation and organization. And this very necessity is confronted with the antiauthoritarian tendencies among the New Left.

These tendencies are difficult to evaluate: they cannot simply be condemned. On the one hand, they are part of the historically correct opposition against the bureaucratic-authoritarian mass parties; on the other hand, they are premature and endanger the effectiveness of the movement. They express, in an abstract form, a distinctive feature of today's radical opposition, namely, the degree to which it draws its force (and truth) from its roots in the whole *individual* and his vital need for a way of life in association with other free individuals, and in a new relation with nature—his own, as well as external nature.

The new individualism raises the problem of the relation between personal and political rebellion, private liberation and social revolution. The inevitable antagonism, the tension between these two, easily collapses into an immediate identification, destroying the potential in both of them. True, no qualitative social change, no socialism, is possible without the emergence of a new rationality *and sensibility* in the individuals themselves: no radical social change without a radical change of the individual agents of change. However, this individual liberation means transcendence beyond the *bourgeois* individual: it means overcoming the bourgeois individual (who is constituted in the tension between personal, private realization and social performance) while at the same time restoring the dimension of the self, of the privacy which the bourgeois culture had once created.

But the bourgeois individual is not overcome by simply refusing social performance, by dropping out and living one's own style of life. To be sure, no revolution without individual liberation, but also no individual liberation without the liberation of society. *Dialectic of liberation*: just as there cannot be any immediate translation of theory into practice, so there cannot be any immediate translation of individual needs and desires into political goals and actions. The tension between the personal and social reality persists; the medium in which the former can affect the latter is still the existing capitalist society. In the formulation of one of the young German radicals, "each of us [radicals] is somehow infested, moronized, saturated, distorted" by the contradictions of the established society. Since the resolution of these contradictions can be the work of only the revolution itself, they have to be borne by the movement, but as *comprehended* contradictions, entering the development of strategy.

No individual and group experiment in liberation can escape this infection by the very system it combats. The infecting agents cannot be pushed aside, they must be combated on their own grounds. This means that, from the beginning, the personal and particular liberation, refusal, withdrawal, must proceed within the political context, defined by the situation in which the radical opposition finds itself, and must continue, in theory and practice, the radical critique of the Establishment within the Establishment; in other words, the individual liberation (refusal) must incorporate the *universal* in the particular protest, and the images and values of a future free society must appear in the personal relationships within the unfree society. For instance, the sexual revolution is no revolution if it does not become a revolution of the human being, if sexual liberation does not converge with political morality. Awareness of the brute fact that, in an unfree society, no particular individual and no particular group can be free must be present in every effort to create conditions of effective refusal to the Establishment.

Objective ambivalence characterizes every movement of the radical opposition—an ambivalence which reflects at one and the same time the power of the Establishment over the whole, and the limits of this power. Co-option threatens the cultural revolution: ecology, rock, ultramodern art are the most conspicuous examples.* Against this threat, the entirely premature immediate identification of private and social freedom

---

* See Chapter 3 below.

creates tranquilizing rather than radicalizing conditions and leads to withdrawal from the political universe in which, alone, freedom can be attained. Perhaps the most serious threat of such appeasement or "pacification" confronts the *communes*.

They continue to be possible nuclei, "cells," laboratories, for testing autonomous, nonalienated relationships. But they are susceptible to isolation and depoliticization. And this means self-co-option or capitulation: the negative which is only the reverse of the affirmative—not its qualitative opposite. Liberation here is having fun within the Establishment, perhaps also with the Establishment, or cheating the Establishment. There is nothing wrong with having fun with the Establishment—but there are situations in which the fun falls flat, becomes silly in any terms because it testifies to political impotence. Under Hitler's fascism, satire became silent: not even Charlie Chaplin and Karl Kraus could keep it up.

Do one's thing, yes, but the time has come to learn that not *any* thing will do, but only those things which testify (no matter how silently) to the intelligence and sensibility of men and women who can do *more* than their own thing, living *and working* for a society without exploitation, among themselves. The distinction between self-indulgence and liberation, between clownery and irony, between criminal gangs and communes (the word itself should be kept sacred!) can be made only by the militants themselves—it cannot be left to the jurisdiction of the courts and the power of the police. To practice this distinction involves self-repression: precursor of revolutionary discipline. Also the good urge to *épater le bourgeois* no longer attains its aim because the traditional "bourgeois" no longer exists, and no "obscenity" or madness can shock a society which has made a blooming business with "obscenity" and has institutionalized madness in its politics and economics.

The fact that the time has come for a self-disciplined organization bears witness not to the defeat but to the prospects of the opposition. The first heroic period of the movement, the period of joyful and often spectacular action, has come to an end. The capitalist enterprise is rapidly approaching its inherent limits on a global scale and is resorting to intensified violence and intensified co-option. Pleasant immediate harmony of one's own thing and the political thing was a token of the weakness of the New Left—as was the so often charming, and necessary, rejection of the *esprit de sérieux*. If the New Left is to continue to grow into a real political force, it will develop its own *esprit de sérieux*, its own rationality in its own sensibility; it will overcome its Oedipus complex on political terms. The standardized use of "pig language," the petty bourgeois anal eroticism, the use of garbage as a weapon against helpless individuals—these are manifestations of a pubertarian revolt against the wrong target. The adversary is no longer represented by the father, or by the boss, or by the professor; the politicians, generals, managers are not fathers, and the people they control are not brothers in revolt. In the society at large, pubertarian rebellion has a short-lived effect; it often seems childish and clownish.

To be sure, the quality of clownishness and childishness easily appears to adhere to authentic acts of protest in situations where the radical opposition is isolated and outrageously weak while the Enemy is almost everywhere and outrageously strong. "Maturity"—by definition—rests with the Establishment, with that which *is,* and the other wisdom then is that of the clown and the child. However, where the protest assumes features which are those of the Establishment itself, of the frustration and repression released by it, this sort of protest is either disregarded, or punished by the authorities with good conscience and wide support on the part of the people.

Of very different political weight are individual and group actions which, although condemned by the Establishment and by the liberals as acts of violence (a grave misnomer compared with the violence practiced by the Establishment), have a transparent educational function in terms of the New Left. Such acts are the disruption of court procedures which clearly expose the class character of the administration of justice; the peaceful occupation of buildings which clearly serve the purposes of the military or of political control; the "heckling" of speakers who clearly espouse the policy of war and oppression. These acts are made punishable under the law, and they are punished with increasing effectiveness. Today, every demonstration is confronted with the ever-present (latent?) violence of suppression: escalation is inherent in the situation. This society strives to impose the principle of nonviolence on the opposition while daily perfecting its own "legitimate" violence, thereby protecting the status quo. Thus the radical opposition faces the problem of the "economy of violence": its own counterviolence is bound to cost dearly, in lives and liberties. What is the political value of sacrifices under these circumstances?

Martyrs have rarely helped a political cause, and "revolutionary suicide" remains suicide. And yet, it would be self-righteous indifference to say that the revolutionary ought to live rather than die for the revolution—an insult to the Communards of all times. Where the Establishment proclaims its professional killers as heroes, and its rebelling victims as criminals, it is hard to save the idea of heroism for the other side. The desperate act, doomed to failure, may for a brief moment tear the veil of justice and expose the faces of brutal suppression; it may arouse the conscience of the neutrals; it may reveal hidden cruelties and lies. Only he who commits the desperate act can judge whether the price he is bound to pay is too high —too high in terms of his own cause as a common cause. Any generalization would be ambivalent, nay, profoundly unjust: it would condemn the victims of the system to the prolonged agony of waiting, to prolonged suffering. But then, the desperate act may have the same result—perhaps a worse result. One is thrown back to the inhuman calculus which an inhuman society imposes: weighing the number of victims and the quantity of their sacrifice against the expected (and reasonably expectable) achievements.

Distinction must be made between violence and revolutionary force. In the counterrevolutionary situation of today, violence is the weapon of the Establishment; it operates everywhere, in the institutions and organizations, in work and fun, on the streets and highways, and in the air. In contrast, the revolutionary force which is destined to terminate this violence does not exist today. Revolutionary force would be the action of masses or classes capable of subverting the established system in order to build a socialist society. Examples would be the unlimited general strike, the occupation and taking over of factories, government buildings, centers of communication and transportation, in coordinated action. In the United States, the conditions for such action do not prevail. The space of operation open to the militant Left is reduced to rigid limits, and the desperate effort to widen it will time and again explode in physical force. This force must be controlled and contained by the movement itself. Action directed toward vague, general, intangible targets is senseless; worse, it augments the number of adversaries. For example: the slogan of the "hot summer" in France, which led to idiotic actions of sabotage and destruction, mostly to the detriment not of the ruling class but of the "people"; or the destruction of the buildings and offices of companies which, in the public mind, are not recognized as "war criminals"; and so on.

VIII

While a "direct democracy" of the majority still remains the form of government or administration for the construction of socialism, "bourgeois democracy" is no longer likely to provide the "field of operations" for the transition to socialism. Nor can it be recaptured where it no longer exists: the totalitarian trend of monopoly capitalism militates against this strategy, and the debunking of its sham-democracy is a part of political countereducation. The latter must, however, take into account what is *authentic* in this sham-democracy, namely, the extent to which it is indeed the integrated, conservative majority that expresses its opinion, chooses between given alternatives, and thus determines policy while the decisions determining the life and death of the people are made by a ruling group beyond popular (and even Congressional) control.*

The dominion of this democracy still leaves room for the building of autonomous local bases. The increasing technological-scientific requirements of production and control make the universities into such a base: first for the system itself, as training schools for its cadres, but also, on the same grounds, schools for the education of future *counter*-cadres. It is still imperative to combat the political inferiority complex widespread among the student movement: the notion that the students are "only" intellectuals, a privileged "elite" and thus a subordinate force which can become effective only if it abandons its own position. This notion is offensive to those who have sacrificed their lives, who continue to risk those lives in every demonstration against the powers that be. If, in the Third World, the students are indeed a revolutionary avant-garde, if they are by the thousands the victims of the terror, then their role in the fight for liberation indicates a feature of the global revolution in the making, namely, the decisive force of a radical consciousness. In the Third World, the militant students directly articulate the rebellion of the people; in the advanced capitalist countries, where they do not (yet) have this

* See *The Pentagon Papers—The Senator Gravel Edition* (Boston: Beacon Press, 1971) for a detailed documentation of this fact.

avant-gardistic function, their privileged position allows (and commits) them to develop such consciousness in theory and practice on their own base—the base of departure for the larger fight. Caught up in its fetishism of labor, the student movement is still reluctant (if not simply refusing) to "admit" that, on the campuses, it has its own base in the infrastructure itself. Moreover, this base extends from the campuses to the economic and political *institutions* where "educated labor" is needed. To be sure, within these institutions, the higher placed cadres will be committed to them, will become part of the hierarchy. But their deteriorating position and chances will weaken this commitment and sharpen the conflict within their education, between the liberating capabilities and the actual servitude of science and technology. However, the solution of this conflict will never be the result of the internal development of science: the new scientific revolution will be part of the social revolution.

To extend the base of the student movement, Rudi Dutschke has proposed the strategy of the *long march through the institutions*: working against the established institutions while working in them, but not simply by "boring from within," rather by "doing the job," learning (how to program and read computers, how to teach at all levels of education, how to use the mass media, how to organize production, how to recognize and eschew planned obsolescence, how to design, et cetera), and at the same time preserving one's own consciousness in working with the others.

The long march includes the concerted effort to build up counterinstitutions. They have long been an aim of the movement, but the lack of funds was greatly responsible for their weakness and their inferior quality. They must be made competitive. This is especially important for the development of radical, "free" *media*. The fact that the radical Left has no equal access to the great chains of information and indoctrination is largely responsible for its isolation. Similarly with the development of independent schools and "free universities." They can be competitive, that is to say, apt to counteract Establishment education, only where they fill a vacuum or where their quality is not only different but also superior. The collection of large funds for the operation of effective counter-institutions requires compromises. The time of the wholesale rejection of the "liberals" has passed—or has not yet come. Radicalism has much to gain from the "legitimate" protest against the war, inflation, and unemployment, from the defense of civil rights—even perhaps from a "lesser evil" in local elections. The ground for the building of a united front is shifting and sometimes dirty—but it is there . . .

I have stressed the key role which the universities play in the present period: they can still function as institutions for the training of counter-cadres. The "restructuring" necessary for the attainment of this goal means more than decisive student participation and nonauthoritarian learning. Making the university "relevant" for today and tomorrow means, instead, presenting the facts and forces that made civilization what it is today and what it could be tomorrow—and that *is* political education. For history indeed repeats itself; it is this repetition of domination and submission that must be halted, and halting it presupposes knowledge of its genesis and of the ways in which it is reproduced: critical thinking.

On this long march, the militant minority has a powerful anonymous ally in the capitalist countries: the deteriorating economic-political conditions of capitalism. True, they may well be the harbinger of a fully developed fascist system, and the New Left should vigorously combat the disastrous notion that this devolopment would accelerate the advent of socialism. The internal contradictions still make for the collapse of capitalism, but a fascist totalitarianism based on the vast resources under capitalist control may well be a stage of this collapse. It would reproduce the contradictions, but on a global scale and in a global space, in which there are still unconquered areas of domination, exploitation, and plunder. The idea of socialism loses its scientific character if its historical necessity is that of an indefinite (and doubtful) future. The objective tendencies make for socialism only to the extent to which the subjective forces struggling for socialism succeed in *bending* them in the direction of socialism—bending them now: today and tomorrow and the days after tomorrow. . . . Capitalism produces its own gravediggers—but their faces may be very different from those of the wretched of the earth, from those of misery and want.

The novel historical pattern of the coming revolution is perhaps best reflected in the role played by a new sensibility in radically changing the "style" of the opposition. I have sketched out this new dimension in *An Essay on Liberation;* here I shall attempt to indicate what is at stake, namely, a new relation between man and nature—his own, and external nature. The radical transformation of nature becomes an integral part of the radical transformation of society. Far from being a mere "psychological" phenomenon in groups or individuals, the new sensibility is the medium in which social change becomes an individual need, the mediation between the political practice of "changing the world" and the drive for personal liberation.

2

NATURE AND REVOLUTION

What is happening is the discovery (or rather, rediscovery) of nature as an ally in the struggle against the exploitative societies in which the violation of nature aggravates the violation of man. The discovery of the liberating forces of nature and their vital role in the construction of a free society becomes a new force in social change.

What is involved in the liberation of nature as a vehicle of the liberation of man?

This notion refers to (1) *human* nature: man's primary impulses and senses as foundation of his rationality and experience and (2) *external* nature: man's existential environment, the "struggle with nature" in which he forms his society. It must be stressed from the beginning that, in both of these manifestations, nature is a historical entity: man encounters nature as transformed by society, subjected to a specific rationality which became, to an ever-increasing extent, technological,

59

instrumentalist rationality, bent to the requirements of capitalism. And this rationality was also brought to bear on man's own nature, on his primary drives. To recall only two characteristic contemporary forms of the adaptation of primary drives to the needs of the established system: the social steering of *aggressiveness* through transferring the aggressive act to technical instruments, thus reducing the sense of guilt; and the social steering of *sexuality* through controlled desublimation, the plastic beauty industry, which leads to a reduction of the sense of guilt and thus promotes "legitimate" satisfaction.

Nature is a part of history, an object of history; therefore, "liberation of nature" cannot mean returning to a pre-technological stage, but advancing to the use of the achievements of technological civilization for freeing man and nature from the destructive abuse of science and technology in the service of exploitation. Then, certain lost qualities of artisan work may well reappear on the new technological base.

In the established society, nature itself, ever more effectively controlled, has in turn become another dimension for the control of man: the extended arm of society and its power. Commercialized nature, polluted nature, militarized nature cut down the life environment of man, not only in an ecological but also in a very existential sense. It blocks the erotic cathexis (and transformation) of his environment: it deprives man from finding himself in nature, beyond and this side of alienation; it also prevents him from recognizing nature as a *subject* in its own right—a subject with which to live in a common human universe. This deprivation is not undone by the opening of nature to massive fun and togetherness, spontaneous as well as organized—a release of frustration which only adds to the violation of nature.

Liberation of nature is the recovery of the life-enhancing forces in nature, the sensuous aesthetic qualities which are foreign to a life wasted in unending competitive performances:

they suggest the new qualities of *freedom*. No wonder then that the "spirit of capitalism" rejects or ridicules the idea of liberated nature, that it relegates this idea to the poetic imagination. Nature, if not left alone and protected as "reservation," is treated in an aggressively scientific way: it is there for the sake of domination; it is value-free matter, material. This notion of nature is a *historical* a priori, pertaining to a specific form of society. A free society may well have a very different a priori and a very different object; the development of the scientific concepts may be grounded in an experience of nature as a totality of life to be protected and "cultivated," and technology would apply this science to the reconstruction of the environment of life.

Domination of man through the domination of nature: the concrete link between the liberation of man and that of nature has become manifest today in the role which the ecology drive plays in the radical movement. The pollution of air and water, the noise, the encroachment of industry and commerce on open natural space have the physical weight of enslavement, imprisonment. The struggle against them is a political struggle; it is obvious to what extent the violation of nature is inseparable from the economy of capitalism. At the same time, however, the political function of ecology is easily "neutralized" and serves the beautification of the Establishment. Still, the physical pollution practiced by the system must be combated here and now—just as its mental pollution. To drive ecology to the point where it is no longer containable within the capitalist framework means first extending the drive *within* the capitalist framework.*

The relation between nature and freedom is rarely made explicit in social theory. In Marxism too, nature is predomi-

---

* See Murray Bookchin, "Ecology and Revolutionary Thought" and "Towards a Liberatory Technology," in *Post-Scarcity Anarchism* (Berkeley: Ramparts Press, 1971).

nantly an object, the adversary in man's "struggle with nature," the field for the ever more rational development of the productive forces.* But in this form, nature appears as that which capitalism has *made* of nature: matter, raw material for the expanding and exploiting administration of men and things. Does this image of nature conform to that of a free society? Is nature only a productive force—or does it also exist *"for its own sake"* and, in *this* mode of existence, for *man?*

In the treatment of *human* nature, Marxism shows a similar tendency to minimize the role of the natural basis in social change—a tendency which contrasts sharply with the earlier writings of Marx. To be sure, "human nature" would be different under socialism to the degree to which men and women would, for the first time in history, develop and fulfill their own needs and faculties in association with each other. But this change is to come about almost as a by-product of the new socialist institutions. Marxist emphasis on the development of political consciousness shows little concern with the roots of liberation in individuals, i.e., with the roots of social relationships there where individuals most directly and profoundly experience their world and themselves: in their *sensibility*, in their instinctual needs.

In *An Essay on Liberation*, I suggested that without a change in this dimension, the old Adam would be reproduced in the new society, and that the construction of a free society *presupposes* a break with the familiar experience of the world: with the mutilated sensibility. Conditioned and "contained" by the rationality of the established system, sense experience tends to "immunize" man against the very unfamiliar experience of the possibilities of human freedom. The development of a radical, nonconformist sensibility assumes vital political importance in view of the unprecedented extent of social con-

---

* See Alfred Schmidt, *Der Begriff der Natur in der Lehre von Marx* (Frankfurt: Europäische Verlagsanstalt, 1962).

trol perfected by advanced capitalism: a control which reaches down into the instinctual and physiological level of existence. Conversely, resistance and rebellion, too, tend to activate and operate on this level.

"Radical sensibility": the concept stresses the active, constitutive role of the senses in shaping reason, that is to say, in shaping the categories under which the world is ordered, experienced, changed. The senses are not merely passive, receptive: they have their own "syntheses" to which they subject the primary data of experience. And these syntheses are not only the pure "forms of intuition" (space and time) which Kant recognized as an inexorable a priori *ordering* of sense data. There are perhaps also other syntheses, far more concrete, far more "material," which may constitute an empirical (i.e., historical) a priori of experience. Our world emerges not only in the pure forms of time and space, but also, and *simultaneously*, as a totality of sensuous qualities—object not only of the eye (synopsis) but of *all* human senses (hearing, smelling, touching, tasting). It is this qualitative, elementary, unconscious, or rather preconscious, constitution of the world of experience, it is this primary experience itself which must change radically if social change is to be radical, qualitative change.

II

The subversive potential of the sensibility, and nature as a field of liberation are central themes in Marx's *Economic and Philosophic Manuscripts*. They have been reread and reinterpreted again and again, but these themes have been largely neglected. Recently, the Manuscripts served to justify the concept of "humanistic socialism" in opposition to the bureaucratic-authoritarian Soviet model; they provided a powerful impetus in the struggle against Stalinism and post-Stalinism. I believe that in spite of their "pre-scientific" character, and in spite of the prevalence of Feuerbach's philosophic naturalism, these writings espouse the most radical and integral idea of socialism, and that precisely here, "nature" finds its place in the theory of revolution.

I recall briefly the principal conception of the Manuscripts. Marx speaks of the "complete emancipation of all human senses and qualities" * as the feature of socialism: only this emancipation is the "transcendence of private property." This means the emergence of a new type of man, different from the human subject of class society in his very nature, in his physiology: "the *senses* of the social man are *other* than those of the non-social man." **

"*Emancipation of the senses*" implies that the senses become "practical" in the reconstruction of society, that they generate new (socialist) relationships between man and man, man and things, man and nature. But the senses become also "sources" of a new (socialist) *rationality*: freed from that of exploitation. The emancipated senses would repel the instrumentalist rationality of capitalism while preserving and developing its achievements. They would attain this goal in two ways: *negatively*—inasmuch as the Ego, the other, and the object world would no longer be experienced in the context of aggressive acquisition, competition, and defensive possession; *positively*—through the "human appropriation of nature," i.e., through the transformation of nature into an environment (medium) for the human being as "species being"; free to develop the specifically human faculties: the creative, aesthetic faculties.

"Only through the objectively unfolded richness of man's essential being is the richness of subjective human sensibility (a musical ear, an eye for beauty of form—in short, *senses* ca-

* Karl Marx, *The Economic and Philosophic Manuscripts of 1844*, Dirk J. Struik, ed. (New York: International Publishers, 1964), p. 139.
** *Ibid.*, p. 141.

pable of human gratification, senses affirming themselves as essential powers of man) either cultivated or brought into being." * The emancipated senses, in conjunction with a natural science proceeding on their basis, would guide the "human appropriation" of nature. Then, nature would have "lost its mere utility," ** it would appear not merely as stuff—organic or inorganic matter—but as life force in its own right, as subject-object;† the striving for life is the substance common to man and nature. Man would then form a living object. The senses would "relate themselves to the thing for the sake of the thing. . . ." †† And they can do so only inasmuch as the thing itself is objectified human *Verhalten*: objectification of human relationships and is thus itself humanly related to man.§

This outrageously unscientific, metaphysical notion foreshadows the mature materialistic theory: it grasps the world of things as objectified human labor, shaped by human labor. Now if this forming human activity produces the technical and natural environment of an acquisitive and repressive society, it will also produce a dehumanized nature; and radical social change will involve a radical transformation of nature.

Also of the *science* of nature? Nature as manifestation of subjectivity: the idea seems inseparable from teleology—long

* *Ibid.*, p. 141.

** *Ibid.*, p. 139.

† "The sun is the object of the plant . . . just as the plant is an object for the sun. . . ." *Ibid.*, p. 181.

†† *Ibid.*, p. 139.

§ "For the sake of the thing"—an illustration:
In Yugoslavia, they sell wooden cutting boards which, on one side, are painted with very colorful, pretty flower patterns; the other side is unpainted. The boards bear the imprint: "don't hurt my pretty face, use other side." Childish anthropomorphism? Certainly. But can we perhaps imagine that the people who had this idea, and those users who pay attention to it, have a quite natural, instinctual aversion against violence and destruction, that they have indeed a "human relation" to matter, that matter to them is part of the *life* environment and thus assumes traits of a living object?

since taboo in Western science. Nature as object per se fitted all too well into the universe of the capitalist treatment of matter to allow discarding the taboo. It seemed entirely justified by the increasingly effective and profitable mastery of nature which was achieved under this taboo.

Is it true that the recognition of nature as a subject is metaphysical teleology incompatible with scientific objectivity? Let us take Jacques Monod's statement of the meaning of objectivity in science:

> What I have tried to show . . . is that the scientific attitude implies what I call the postulate of objectivity—that is to say, the fundamental postulate that there is no plan, that there is no intention in the universe.*

The idea of the liberation of nature stipulates no such plan or intention in the universe: liberation is the possible plan and intention of human beings, brought to bear upon nature. However, it does stipulate that nature is susceptible to such an undertaking, and that there are forces in nature which have been distorted and suppressed—forces which could support and enhance the liberation of man. This capacity of nature may be called "chance," or "blind freedom," and it may give good meaning to the human effort to redeem this blindness—in Adorno's words: to help nature "to open its eyes," to help it "on the poor earth to become what perhaps it would like to be." **

Nature as subject without teleology, without "plan" and "intention": this notion goes well with Kant's "purposiveness without purpose." The most advanced concepts of the Third

* Interview with the *New York Times,* March 15, 1971.
** Theodor W. Adorno, *Aesthetische Theorie* (Frankfurt/Main: Suhrkamp, 1970), pp. 100, 107.

Critique have not yet been explored in their truly revolutionary significance. The aesthetic form in art has the aesthetic form in nature (*das Naturschöne*) as its correlate, or rather desideratum. If the idea of beauty pertains to nature as well as to art, this is not merely an analogy, or a human idea imposed on nature—it is the insight that the aesthetic form, as a token of freedom, is a mode (or moment?) of existence of the human as well as the natural universe, an objective quality. Thus Kant attributes the beautiful in nature to nature's "capacity to form itself, in its freedom, also in an aesthetically purposive way, according to chemical laws. . . ." *

The Marxian conception understands nature as a universe which becomes the congenial medium for human gratification to the degree to which nature's *own* gratifying forces and qualities are recovered and released. In sharp contrast to the capitalist exploitation of nature, its "human appropriation" would be nonviolent, nondestructive: oriented on the life-enhancing, sensuous, aesthetic qualities inherent in nature. Thus transformed, "humanized," nature would respond to man's striving for fulfillment, nay, the latter would not be possible without the former. Things have their "inherent measure" (*inhärentes Mass*):** this measure is *in* them, is the potential enclosed in them; only man can free it and, in doing so, free his own human potential. Man is the only being who can "form things in accordance with the laws of beauty." †

Aesthetics of liberation, beauty as a "form" of freedom: it looks as if Marx has shied away from this anthropomorphist, idealistic conception. Or is this apparently idealistic notion rather the *enlargement of the materialistic base?* For "man is directly a *natural being*; he is a corporeal, living, real, sensuous,

* *Critique of Judgment,* S 58.
** Marx, *loc. cit.,* p. 114.
† *Ibid.*

objective being" who has "real, sensuous objects" as the objects of his life.* And his senses ("like those organs which are directly social in their form")** are active, practical in the "appropriation" of the object world; they express the social existence of man, his "objectification." This is no longer Feuerbach's "naturalism" but, on the contrary, the extension of Historical Materialism to a dimension which is to play a vital role in the liberation of man.

There is, however, a definite internal limit to the idea of the liberation of nature through "human appropriation." True, the aesthetic dimension is a vital dimension of freedom; true, it repels violence, cruelty, brutality, and by this token will become an essential quality of a free society, not as a separate realm of "higher culture," but as a driving force and *motive* in the *construction* of such a society. And yet, certain brute facts, unconquered and perhaps unconquerable facts, call for skepticism. Can the human appropriation of nature ever achieve the elimination of violence, cruelty, and brutality in the daily sacrifice of animal life for the physical reproduction of the human race? To treat nature "for its own sake" sounds good, but it is certainly not for the sake of the animal to be eaten, nor probably for the sake of the plant. The end of this war, the perfect peace in the animal world—this idea belongs to the Orphic myth, not to any conceivable historical reality. In the face of the suffering inflicted by man on man, it seems terribly "premature" to campaign for universal vegetarianism or synthetic foodstuffs; as the world is, priority must be on *human* solidarity among human beings. And yet, no free society is imaginable which does not, under its "regulative idea of reason," make the concerted effort to reduce consistently the suffering which man imposes on the animal world.

Marx's notion of a human appropriation of nature retains

* *Ibid.*, p. 181.
** *Ibid.*, p. 139.

something of the *hubris* of domination. "Appropriation," no matter how human, remains appropriation of a (living) object by a subject. It offends that which is essentially other than the appropriating subject, and which exists precisely as object in its own right—that is, as subject! The latter may well be hostile to man, in which case the relation would be one of struggle; but the struggle may also subside and make room for peace, tranquillity, fulfillment. In this case, not appropriation but rather its negation would be the nonexploitative relation: surrender, "letting-be," acceptance . . . But such surrender meets with the impenetrable resistance of matter; nature is not a manifestation of "spirit," but rather its essential *limit*.

III

Although the historical concept of nature as a dimension of social change does not imply teleology and does not attribute a "plan" to nature, it does conceive of nature as subject-object: as a *cosmos* with its own potentialities, necessities, and chances. And these potentialities can be, not only in the sense of their value-free function in theory and practice, but also as bearers of *objective values*. These are envisaged in such phrases as "violation of nature," "suppression of nature." Violation and suppression then mean that human action against nature, man's interrelation with nature, offends against certain objective *qualities* of nature—qualities which are essential to the enhancement and fulfillment of life. And it is on such objective grounds that the liberation for man to his own humane faculties is linked to the liberation of nature—that "truth" is attributable to nature not only in a mathematical but also in an existential sense. The emancipation of man involves the recognition of such truth in things, in nature. The Marxian vision recaptures the ancient theory of knowledge as *recollection:* "science" as the *re*discovery of the true *Forms* of things, distorted and denied in the established reality, the perpetual *materialistic core of idealism.* The "idea," as the term for these Forms, is not a "mere" idea, but an image illuminating what is false, distorted in the way in which things are "given," what is missing in their familiar perception, in the mutilated experience which is the work of society.

Recollection thus is not remembrance of a Golden Past (which never existed), of childhood innocence, primitive man, et cetera. Recollection as epistemological faculty rather is synthesis, reassembling the bits and fragments which can be found in the distorted humanity and distorted nature. This recollected material has become the domain of the imagination, it has been sanctioned by the repressive societies in art, and as "poetic truth"—poetic truth only, and therefore not much good in the actual transformation of society. These images may well be called "innate ideas" inasmuch as they cannot possibly be given in the immediate experience which prevails in the repressive societies. They are given rather as the *horizon* of experience under which the immediately given forms of things appear as "negative," as denial of their inherent possibilities, their truth. But in this sense, they are "innate" in man as *historical* being; they are themselves historical because the possibilities of liberation are always and everywhere historical possibilities. Imagination, *as knowledge,* retains the insoluble tension between idea and reality, the potential and the actual. This is the *idealistic core* of dialectical materialism: the transcendence of freedom beyond the given forms. In this sense too, Marxian theory is the historical heir of German Idealism.

Freedom thus becomes a "regulative concept of reason" guiding the practice of changing reality in accordance with its "idea," i.e., its own potentialities—to make reality free for its truth. Dialectical materialism understands freedom as historical, empirical transcendence, as a force of social change, transcending its immediate form also in a socialist society—not toward ever more production, not toward Heaven or Paradise, but toward an ever more peaceful, joyful struggle with the inexorable resistance of society and nature. This is the philosophical core of the theory of the permanent revolution.

As such force, freedom is rooted in the primary drives of men and women, it is the vital need to enhance their life instincts. Prerequisite is the capacity of the senses to experience not only the "given" but also the "hidden" qualities of things which would make for the betterment of life. The radical redefinition of sensibility as "practical" desublimates the idea of freedom without abandoning its transcendent content: the senses are not only the basis for the *epistemological* constitution of reality, but also for its *transformation,* its *subversion* in the interest of liberation.

Human freedom is thus rooted in the human *sensibility*: the senses do not only "receive" what is given to them, in the form in which it appears, they do not "delegate" the transformation of the given to another faculty (the understanding); rather, they discover or *can* discover by themselves, in their "practice," new (more gratifying) possibilities and capabilities, forms and qualities of things, and can urge and guide their realization. The emancipation of the senses would make freedom what it is not yet: a sensuous need, an objective of the Life Instincts (*Eros*).

In a society based on alienated labor, human sensibility is *blunted*: men perceive things only in the forms and functions in which they are given, made, used by the existing society; and they perceive only the possibilities of transformation as defined by, and confined to, the existing society.* Thus, the existing society is *reproduced* not only in the mind, the consciousness of men, but *also in their senses*; and no persuasion,

---

* For the following see my *An Essay on Liberation* (Boston: Beacon Press, 1969), pp. 36 ff.

no theory, no reasoning can break this prison, unless the fixed, petrified *sensibility* of the individuals is *"dissolved," opened* to *a new dimension of history,* until the oppressive familiarity with the given object world is broken—broken in a *second alienation:* that from the alienated society.

Today, in the revolt against the "consumer society," sensibility strives to become "practical," the vehicle for radical reconstruction, for new ways of life. It has become a force in the *political* struggle for liberation.* And that means: the individual emancipation of the senses is supposed to be the beginning, even the foundation, of *universal* liberation, the free society is to take roots in new instinctual needs. How is this possible? How can "humanity," human solidarity as *"concrete universal"* (and not as abstract value), as real force, as "praxis," originate in the individual sensibility; how can objective freedom originate in the most subjective faculties of man?

We are faced with the *dialectic* of the universal and the particular: how can the human sensibility, which is *principium individuationis,* also generate a *universalizing* principle?

I refer again to the philosophical treatment of this problem in German idealism: here is the intellectual origin of the Marxian concept. For *Kant:* a universal sensorium (the pure forms of intuition) constitutes the one unified framework of sense experience, thus validating the universal categories of the understanding. For *Hegel:* reflection on the content and mode of *my* immediate sense certainty reveals the "We" in the "I" of intuition and perception. When the still unreflected consciousness has reached the point where it becomes conscious of itself and its relation to its objects, where it has experienced a "trans-sensible" world "behind" the sensuous appearance of things, it discovers that *we* ourselves are behind the curtain of

---

* The fight for the Peoples Park in Berkeley, which was met with brute force by the armed guardians of law and order, shows the explosion of sensibility in political action.

appearance. And this "we" unfolds as social reality in the struggle between Master and Servant for "mutual recognition."

This is the turning point on the road that leads from Kant's effort to reconcile man and nature, freedom and necessity, universal and particular, to Marx's materialistic solution: Hegel's *Phenomenology* breaks with Kant's transcendental conception: history and society enter into the theory of knowledge (and into the very structure of knowledge) and do away with the "purity" of the a priori; the materialization of the idea of freedom begins. But a closer look shows that the same tendency was already present in Kant's philosophy: in the development from the First to the Third Critique.

1) In the *First Critique,* the freedom of the subject is present only in the epistemological syntheses of the sense data; freedom is relegated to the transcendental Ego's pure syntheses: it is the power of the a priori by virtue of which the transcendental subject constitutes the objective world of experience; theoretical knowledge.

2) In the *Second Critique,* the realm of *praxis* is reached with the stipulation of the autonomy of the moral person: his power to *originate* causation without breaking the universal causation which governs nature: necessity. The price: subjection of the sensibility to the categorical imperative of reason. The relation between human freedom and natural necessity remains obscure.

3) In the *Third Critique,* man and nature are joined in the aesthetic dimension, the rigid "otherness" of nature is reduced, and Beauty appears as "symbol of morality." The union of the realm of freedom and that of necessity is here conceived not as the mastery of nature, not as bending nature to the purposes of man, but as attributing to nature an ideal purposiveness "of its own: a purposiveness without purpose."

But it is only the *Marxian* conception which, while preserving the critical, transcendent element of idealism, uncovers

the material, historical ground for the reconciliation of human
freedom and natural necessity; subjective and objective freedom. This union presupposes liberation: the revolutionary
praxis which is to abolish the institutions of capitalism and to
replace them by socialist institutions and relationships. But in
this transition, the emancipation of the senses must accompany
the emancipation of consciousness, thus involving the *totality*
of human existence. The individuals themselves must change
in their very instincts and sensibilities if they are to build, in
association, a *qualitatively* different society. But why the emphasis on *aesthetic* needs in this reconstruction?

IV

It is not just in passing and out of exuberance that Marx speaks
of the formation of the object world "in accordance with the
laws of beauty" as a feature of free human practice. Aesthetic
qualities are essentially nonviolent, nondomineering (I shall
come back to it in Chapter III)—qualities which, in the domain
of the arts, and in the repressive use of the term "aesthetic" as
pertaining to the sublimated "higher culture" only, are divorced
from the social reality and from "practice" as such. The revolution would undo this repression and recapture aesthetic needs
as a subversive force, capable of counteracting the dominating
aggressiveness which has shaped the social and natural universe. The faculty of being "receptive," "passive," is a precondition of freedom: it is the ability to see things in their own
right, to experience the joy enclosed in them, the erotic energy
of nature—an energy which is there to be liberated; nature,
too, awaits the revolution! This receptivity is itself the soil
of creation: it is opposed, not to productivity, but to *destructive* productivity.

The latter has been the ever more conspicuous feature of
male domination; inasmuch as the "male principle" has been

the ruling mental and physical force, a free society would be the "definite negation" of this principle—it would be a *female* society. In this sense, it has nothing to do with matriarchy of any sort; the image of the woman as mother is itself repressive; it transforms a biological fact into an ethical and cultural value and thus it supports and justifies her social repression. At stake is rather the ascent of Eros over aggression, in men *and* women; and this means, in a male-dominated civilization, the "femalization" of the male. It would express the decisive change in the instinctual structure: the weakening of primary aggressiveness which, by a combination of biological and social factors, has governed the patriarchal culture.

In this transformation, the Women's Liberation Movement becomes a radical force to the degree to which it transcends the entire sphere of aggressive needs and performances, the entire social organization and division of functions. In other words, the movement becomes radical to the degree to which it aims, not only at equality *within* the job and value structure of the *established* society (which would be the equality of dehumanization) but rather at a change in the structure itself (the basic demands of equal opportunity, equal pay, and release from full-time household and child care are a prerequisite). Within the established structure, neither men nor women are free—and the dehumanization of men may well be greater than that of women since the former suffer not only the conveyor belt and assembly line but also the standards and "ethics" of the "business community."

And yet, the liberation of women would be more sweeping than that of men because the repression of women has been constantly fortified by the social use of their biological constitution. The bearing of children, being a mother, is supposed to be not only their natural function but also the fulfillment of their "nature"—and so is being a wife, since the reproduction of the species occurs within the framework of the monogamous patriarchal family. Outside this framework, the woman is still predominantly a plaything or a temporary outlet for sexual energy not consummated in marriage.

Marxian theory considers sexual exploitation as the primary, original exploitation, and the Women's Liberation Movement fights the degradation of the woman to a "sexual object." But it is difficult to overcome the feeling that here, repressive qualities characteristic of the bourgeois-capitalist organization of society enter into the fight against this organization. Historically, the image of the woman as sexual object, and her exchange value on the market, devalue the earlier repressive images of the woman as mother and wife. These earlier images were essential to the bourgeois ideology during a period of capitalist development now left behind: the period where some "inner-worldly asceticism" was still operative in the dynamic of the economy. In comparison, the present image of the woman as sexual object is a *desublimation* of bourgeois morality —characteristic of a "higher stage" of capitalist development. Here, too, the commodity form is universalized: it now invades formerly sanctified and protected realms. The (female) body, as seen and plastically idealized by *Playboy*, becomes desirable merchandise with a high exchange value. Disintegration of bourgeois morality, perhaps—but *cui bono?* To be sure, this new body image promotes sales, and the plastic beauty may not be the real thing, but they stimulate aesthetic-sensuous needs which, in their development, must become incompatible with the body as instrument of alienated labor. The male body, too, is made the object of sexual image creation—also plasticized and deodorized . . . clean exchange value. After the secularization of religion, after the transformation of ethics into Orwellian hypocrisy—is the "socialization" of the body as sexual object perhaps one of the last decisive steps toward the completion of the exchange society: the completion which is the beginning of the end?

Still, the publicity with the body (at present, the female body) as object is dehumanizing, the more so since it plays up to the dominant male as the aggressive subject for whom the female is there, to be taken, to be laid. It is in the nature of sexual relationships that both, male and female, are object *and* subject at the same time; erotic and aggressive energy are fused in both. The surplus-aggression of the male is socially conditioned—as is the surplus-passivity of the female. But beneath the social factors which determine male aggressiveness and female receptivity, a *natural* contrast exists: it is the woman who "embodies," in a literal sense, the promise of peace, of joy, of the end of violence. Tenderness, receptivity, sensuousness have become features (or mutilated features) of her body —features of her (repressed) humanity. These female qualities may well be socially determined by the development of capitalism. The process is truly dialectical.* Although the reduction of the concrete individual faculties to abstract labor power established an abstract equality between men and women (equality before the machine), this abstraction was less complete in the case of women. They were employed in the material process of production to a lesser extent than men. Women were fully employed in the household, the family, which was supposed to be the sphere of realization for the bourgeois individual. However, this sphere was isolated from the productive process and thus contributed to the women's mutilation. And yet, this isolation (separation) from the alienated work world of capitalism enabled the woman to remain less brutalized by the Performance Principle, to remain closer to her sensibility: more human than men. That this image (and reality) of the woman has been determined by an aggressive, male-dominated society does not mean that this determination must be re-

* This dialectic is the center of Angela Davis's paper *Marxism and Women's Liberation* (not yet published). Written in jail, this paper is the work of a great woman, militant, intellectual.

jected, that the liberation of women must overcome the female "nature." This equalization of male and female would be regressive: it would be a new form of female acceptance of a male principle. Here too the historical process is dialectical: the patriarchal society has created a female image, a female counter-force, which may still become one of the gravediggers of patriarchal society. In this sense too, the woman holds the promise of liberation. It is the woman who, in Delacroix' painting, holding the flag of the revolution, leads the people on the barricades. She wears no uniform; her breasts are bare, and her beautiful face shows no trace of violence. But she has a rifle in her hand—for the end of violence is still to be fought for . . .

*". . . certain periods of highest development of art stand in
no direct connection with the general development of society,
nor with the material basis and the skeleton structure of its
organization."* MARX

I

Cultural Revolution: the phrase, in the West, first suggests that
ideological developments are ahead of developments at the
base of society: cultural revolution but *not* (yet) political and
economic revolution. While, in
the arts, in literature and music,
in communication, in the mores
and fashions, changes have occurred which suggest a new experience, a radical transformation of values, the social structure and its political expressions
seem to remain basically un-
changed, or at least to lag be-

3

**ART AND
REVOLUTION**

hind the cultural changes. But "Cultural Revolution" also suggests that the radical opposition today involves in a new sense
the entire realm beyond that of the material needs—nay, that it
aims at a total transformation of the entire traditional culture.

The strong emphasis on the political potential of the arts
which is a feature of this radicalism is first of all expressive
of the need for an effective *communication* of the indictment
of the established reality and of the goals of liberation. It is
the effort to find forms of communication that may break the
oppressive rule of the established language and images over
the mind and body of man—language and images which have
long since become a means of domination, indoctrination, and
deception. Communication of the radically nonconformist, new
historical goals of the revolution requires an equally noncon-

79

formist language (in the widest sense), a language that reaches a population which has introjected the needs and values of their masters and managers and made them their own, thus reproducing the established system in their minds, their consciousness, their senses and instincts. Such a new language, if it is to be political, cannot possibly be "invented": it will necessarily depend on the subverting use of traditional material, and the possibilities of this subversion are naturally sought where the tradition itself has permitted, sanctioned, and preserved another language, and other images. Such other languages exist mainly in two domains at opposite poles of society:

    1) in art *

    2) in the folk tradition (black language, argot, slang)

The latter is largely the language of the oppressed, and as such it has a natural affinity to protest and refusal. In black language, methodically fostered by black people today, it strengthens solidarity, the consciousness of their identity, and of their repressed or distorted cultural tradition. And because of this function, it militates against generalization. Another form of linguistic rebellion is the systematic use of "obscenities." I stressed its supposed political potential (in *An Essay on Liberation,* p. 35); today, this potential is already ineffective. Spoken to an Establishment which can well afford "obscenity," this language no longer identifies the radical, the one who does not belong. Moreover, standardized obscene language is repressive desublimation: facile (though vicarious) gratification of aggressiveness. It turns easily against sexuality itself. The verbalization of the genital and anal sphere, which has become a ritual in left-radical speech (the "obligatory" use of "fuck," "shit") is a *debasement* of sexuality. If a radical says, "Fuck Nixon," he associates the word for highest genital gratification

* I use the term "art" to include literature and music.

with the highest representative of the oppressive Establishment, and "shit" for the products of the Enemy takes over the bourgeois rejection of anal eroticism. In this (totally unconscious) debasement of sexuality, the radical seems to punish himself for his lack of power; his language is losing its political impact. And while serving as a shibboleth of identity (belonging to the radical nonconformists), this linguistic rebellion mars the *political* identity by the mere verbalization of petty bourgeois taboos.

At the other pole of society, in the domain of the arts, the tradition of protest, the negation of that which is "given," persists in its own universe and in its own right. Here, the other language, the other images continue to be communicated, to be heard and seen; and it is this art which, in a subverted form, is now being used as a weapon in the political fight against the established society—with an impact far transcending a specific privileged or underprivileged group. The subverting use of the artistic tradition aims from the beginning at a systematic *desublimation* of culture: that is to say, at undoing the aesthetic form.* "Aesthetic form" means the total of qualities (harmony, rhythm, contrast) which make an oeuvre a self-contained whole, with a structure and order of its own (the style). By virtue of these qualities the work of art *transforms* the order prevailing in reality. This transformation is "illusion," but an illusion which gives the contents represented a meaning and a function different from those they have in the prevailing universe of discourse. Words, sounds, images, from another dimension "bracket" and invalidate the right of the established reality for the sake of a reconciliation still to come.

The harmonizing illusion, the idealistic transfiguration, and, with it, *the divorce of the arts from reality* has been a feature of this aesthetic form. Its desublimation means: return to

* See *An Essay on Liberation, loc. cit.,* pp. 42 f.

an "immediate" art, which responds to, and activates, not only the intellect and a refined, "distilled," restricted sensibility, but also, and primarily, a *natural* sense experience freed from the requirements of an obsolescent exploitative society. The search is for art forms which express the experience of the body (*and* the "soul"), not as vehicles of labor power and resignation, but as vehicles of liberation. This is the search for a *sensuous culture,* "sensuous" inasmuch as it involves the radical transformation of man's sense experience and receptivity: their emancipation from a self-propelling, profitable, and mutilating productivity. But the cultural revolution goes far beyond a revaluation in the arts: it strikes at the roots of capitalism in the individuals themselves.

In the preceding chapter, I have tried to outline the material, practical force of this emancipation. Cultural changes can no longer be adequately understood within the abstract schema of base and superstructure (ideology). At the present stage, the disintegration of "bourgeois culture" affects the *operational* values of capitalism. A new experience of reality, new values weaken the conformity among the underlying population. More effectively than its political goals and slogans, this "existential" protest, hard to isolate and hard to punish, threatens the cohesion of the social system. And it is this protest which motivates the efforts to subvert also the "higher" culture of the system: the striving for essentially different ways of life seems to depend largely on liberation from "bourgeois culture."

Today, the break with the bourgeois tradition in art, serious as well as popular, seems to be all but complete. The new "open" forms or "free forms" express not just a new style in the historical succession but rather the negation of the very universe in which art has moved, the efforts to change the historical function of art. Are these efforts really steps on the road to liberation? Do they really subvert what they are supposed to subvert? To prepare the answer, the target has first to be brought into focus.

"*Bourgeois culture*": is there a meaningful common denominator (other than a vague unhistorical one) which characterizes the dominant culture from the 16th to the 20th centuries? The historical subject of this culture is the *bourgeoisie:* first the urban middle class between the nobility and the agricultural and manufacturing laborers; subsequently the ruling class confronting the industrial working class during the 19th century. *But* the bourgeoisie which is (supposed to be) represented by the culture of this period, this bourgeoisie is, in terms of its social function and spirit, *no longer* the *ruling class* today, and its culture is no longer the culture dominating the advanced capitalist society today: neither the *material* nor the *intellectual,* artistic ("higher") culture.

The *distinction* between these two spheres of culture must be recalled:

—the material culture comprising the actual patterns of behavior in "earning a living," the system of *operational* values; the rule of the Performance Principle; the patriarchal family as educational unit; work as calling, vocation;

—the intellectual culture comprising the "higher values," science and the "humanities," the arts, religion.

We shall see that these two dimensions of bourgeois culture, far from constituting a unified whole, have developed in tension, even contradiction, to each other.

In the *material culture,* typically "bourgeois" have been:

—the preoccupation with money, business, "commerce" as "existential" value, with religious and ethical sanction;

—the dominant economic and "spiritual" function of the father as head of the family *and* of the enterprise; and

—an authoritarian education designed to reproduce and introject these utilitarian goals.

This whole "life style" of bourgeois materialism was permeated with an instrumentalist rationality which militated against libertarian tendencies, debased sex, discriminated against women, and imposed repression for the sake of God and business.

At the same time the *intellectual culture*, devaluing and even negating this material culture, was largely idealistic: it sublimated the repressive forces by joining inexorably fulfillment and renunciation, freedom and submission, beauty and illusion (*Schein*).

Now it is rather obvious that this has ceased to be the dominant culture. Today, the ruling class has neither a culture of its own (so that the ideas of the ruling class could become the ruling ideas) nor does it practice the bourgeois culture it has inherited. The classical bourgeois culture is outdated now, it is disintegrating—not under the impact of the cultural revolution and the student rebellion, but rather by virtue of the dynamic of monopoly capitalism which made this culture incompatible with the requirements of its survival and growth.

I shall briefly recapitulate the most general indices of this internal *disintegration* of bourgeois culture:

—the reversal of "inner-worldly asceticism" as the classical "spirit of capitalism": the "Keynesian revolution" as a requisite of enlarged capital accumulation;

—the dependence of the ruling class on the reproduction of a "consumer society" which comes into increasing contradiction to the capitalist need for the perpetuation of alienated labor;

—in line with the social need for an intensive integration of behavior into the capitalist orbit: discreditation of idealistic notions, education to positivism, ingression of the methods of the "hard" sciences into the social sciences and humanities;

—the co-option of libertarian subcultures which can enlarge the commodity market; and

—the destruction of the universe of language: super-Orwellianism as normal communication (see p. 109 below);

—the decline of the father image and of the Superego in the bourgeois family.*

Where and when today's ruling class still adheres to the traditional cultural values, it is with the ritual cynicism with which one speaks of defending the Free World, private enterprise, civil rights, individualism. Cynicism: because no ideology can possibly conceal the fact that this ruling class is no longer developing the productive forces once contained in these institutions but is arresting and abusing them. The ideology retreats from the superstructure (where it is replaced by a system of blatant lies and non-sense) and becomes incorporated in the goods and services of the consumer society; they sustain the false consciousness of the good life.

Now the question arises: if today we are witnessing a disintegration of bourgeois culture which is the work of the internal dynamic of contemporary capitalism and the adjustment of culture to the requirements of contemporary capitalism, is not the cultural revolution then, inasmuch as it aims at the destruction of bourgeois culture, falling in line with the capitalist adjustment and redefinition of culture? Is it not thus defeating its own purpose, namely, to prepare the soil for a qualitatively different, a radically anticapitalist culture? Is there not a dangerous divergence, if not contradiction, between the political goals of the rebellion and its cultural theory and praxis? And must not the rebellion change its cultural "strategy" in order to resolve this contradiction?

The contradiction appears most clearly in the efforts to develop an anti-art, "living art"—in the rejection of the aesthetic

* See *Eros and Civilization* (Boston: Beacon Press, 1955, 1966), pp. 85 ff.; and Henry and Yela Lowenfeld, "Our Permissive Society and the Superego," in *The Psychoanalytic Quarterly*, October 1970.

form. These efforts are to serve the larger long-range aim: to undo the separation of the intellectual from the material culture, a separation which is said to express the class character of bourgeois culture. And this class character is held to be constitutive in the most representative and most perfect *oeuvres* of the bourgeois period.

First, a brief critical look at this notion. A survey of these *oeuvres* at least since the 19th century would show that a thoroughly *antibourgeois* stance is prevalent: the higher culture indicts, rejects, withdraws from the material culture of the bourgeoisie. It is indeed separated; it dissociates *itself* from the world of commodities, from the brutality of bourgeois industry and commerce, from the distortion of human relationships, from capitalist materialism, from instrumentalist reason. The aesthetic universe *contradicts* reality—a "methodical," intentional contradiction.

This contradiction is never "direct," immediate, total; it does not assume the form of a social or political novel, poem, painting, et cetera. Or, when it does (as in the work of Büchner, Zola, Ibsen, Brecht, Delacroix, Daumier, Picasso), the *oeuvre* remains committed to the structure of *art*, to the *form* of the drama, the novel, the painting, thereby articulating the distance from reality. The negation is "contained" by the form, it is always a "broken," "sublimated" contradiction, which transfigures, transsubstantiates the given reality—and the liberation from it. This transfiguration creates a universe closed on itself; no matter how realistic, naturalistic, it remains *the other* of reality and nature. And in this aesthetic universe, the contradictions are indeed "solved" inasmuch as they appear within a universal order to which they belong. And this universal order is first a very concrete, historical one: that of the Greek city state, or the feudal courts, or bourgeois society. In this universe, the fate of the individual (as depicted in the

work of art) is more than individual: it is also that of others.
There is no work of art where this universal does not show
forth in the particular configurations, actions, sufferings.
"Shows forth" in an immediate, sensuous rather than "symbolic" form: the individual "embodies" the universal; thus he
becomes the harbinger of a universal truth which erupts in his
unique fate and place.

The work of art first transforms a particular, individual content into the universal social order of which it partakes—but
does the transformation *terminate* in this order? Is the truth, the
"validity," of the work of art *confined* to the Greek city state,
bourgeois society, and so on? Evidently not. Aesthetic theory is
confronted with the age-old question: what are the qualities
which make the Greek tragedy, the medieval epic still true
today—not only understandable but also enjoyable today? The
answer must be sought on two levels of "objectivity": (1) the
aesthetic transformation reveals the human condition as it pertains to the entire history (Marx: pre-history) of mankind over
and above any specific condition, and (2) the aesthetic form
responds to certain constant qualities of the human intellect,
sensibility, and imagination—qualities which the tradition of
philosophical aesthetics has interpreted as the idea of beauty.*

By virtue of this transformation of the specific historical
universe in the work of art—a transformation which arises in the
presentation of the specific content itself—art opens the established reality to another dimension: that of possible liberation.
To be sure, this is illusion, *Schein,* but an illusion in which another reality shows forth. And it does so only if art *wills* itself
as illusion: as an unreal world other than the established one.
And precisely in this transfiguration, art preserves and *tran-*

* For an analysis of the discussion of the "objectivist position in
aesthetics" see Stefan Morawski, "Artistic Value," in *The Journal of
Aesthetic Education,* vol. 5, no. 1, especially pp. 36 ff.

scends its class character. And transcends it, not toward a realm of mere fiction and fantasy, but toward a universe of concrete possibilities.

I shall try first to isolate the features which appear as typical of the class character of the higher culture of the bourgeois period. They are generally seen in the discovery and celebration of the individual *subject*, the "autonomous person" which is to come into its own, to become a self in and against a world that destroys the self. This subjectivity opens the new dimension in the bourgeois reality, a dimension of freedom and fulfillment; but this realm of freedom is finally found in the *inner* being (*Innerlichkeit*) and is thus "sublimated," if not made unreal. In the given reality, the individual accommodates himself, or renounces, or destroys himself. The given reality exists in its own right, its own truth; it has its own ethics, its own happiness and pleasures (and much can be said for them!). The other truth is music, song, verse, image, in the work of the masters: an aesthetic realm, self-sufficient, a world of aesthetic harmony which leaves the miserable reality to its own devices. It is precisely this "inner truth," this sublime beauty, depth, and harmony of the aesthetic imagery, which today appears as mentally and physically intolerable, false, as part of the commodity culture, as an obstacle to liberation.

I confess that I have difficulties in defining the specific class character of bourgeois art. To be sure, the works of bourgeois art are commodities; they may even have been created as commodities for sale on the market. But this fact by itself does not change their substance, their truth. "Truth" in art refers not only to the internal consistency and logic of the *oeuvre*, but also to the *validity* of what it says, of its images, sound, rhythm. They reveal and communicate facts and possibilities of the human existence; they "see" this existence in a light very different from that in which reality appears in ordinary (and scientific) language and communication. In this sense, the authentic *oeuvre* has indeed a meaning which claims general validity, objectivity. After all, there is such a thing as the text, the structure, the rhythm of a work which is there, "objectively," and which can be reconstructed and identified as being there, identical in, through, and against all particular interpretation, reception, distortion. Nor is this objectivity of the *oeuvre*, its general validity, canceled by the fact that those who created it have come from bourgeois families: a confusion of the psychological and ontological realm. To be sure, the ontological structure of art is a *historical* one, but history is the history of *all* classes. They share an environment which is the same in its general features (town, countryside, nature, seasons, et cetera), and their struggle takes place within this universal objective environment.

Moreover, art envisions still another, larger, as it were, "negative," totality: the "tragic" universe of the human existence and of the ever-renewed quest for secular redemption— the promise of liberation. I suggested that art invokes this promise and, by virtue of this function, transcends all particular class content without, however, eliminating it. Evidently, there is such a particular class content in bourgeois art: the bourgeois, his décor, and his problems dominate the scene, as the knight, his décor, and his problems do in medieval art; but does this fact suffice to define the truth, the content, and form of the work of art? Hegel has revealed the continuity of substance, the truth which joins the modern novel and the medieval epic:

> [The] spirit of modern fiction is, in fact, that of chivalry, once more taken seriously and receiving a true content. The contingent character of external existence has changed to a stable, secure order of civic society and the state, so that now the police, the courts of law, the army and the government take the

place of those chimerical objects which the knight of chivalry proposed to himself. For this reason, the knightly character of the heroes who play their parts in our modern novels is altered. They appear before us as individuals whose subjective aims of love, honor, ambition, or ideas of world reform are confronted by this established order and the ordinary prose of life which present obstacles on every side. The result is that subjective desires and demands rise to unfathomable heights. Everyone finds himself face to face with an enchanted (*verzauberte,* mystified) world—a world which is unsuitable (*ungehörig,* alien) for him, which he must combat because it resists him and in its tenacious stability refuses to give way before his passions, but interposes as an obstacle the will of a father, an aunt, bourgeois conditions, etc.*

Certainly, there are conflicts and solutions which are specifically bourgeois, foreign to preceding historical periods (see Defoe, Lessing, Flaubert, Dickens, Ibsen, Thomas Mann), but their specific character is loaded with universal meaning. Similarly, are Tristan, Parsival, Siegfried just feudal knights whose fate is simply due to the feudal code? Obviously, the class content is there, but it becomes transparent as the condition and as the dream of humanity: conflict and reconciliation between man and man, man and nature—the miracle of the aesthetic form. In the particular content appears another dimension where the (feudal and) bourgeois men and women incarnate the species man: the human being.

To be sure, the higher culture of the bourgeois period was

* Hegel, *Vorlesungen über die Aesthetik* (*Sämmtliche Werke*), Glockner, ed. (Stuttgart: Frommann, 1928), vol. XIII, pp. 215 f. Translation by F. P. R. Osmaston, *The Philosophy of Fine Art* (London: G. Bell and Sons, 1920), vol. II, p. 375 (slight changes by me).

(and is) an elitist culture, available and even meaningful only to a privileged minority—but this character it shares with all culture since antiquity. The inferior place (or absence) of the laboring classes in this cultural universe certainly makes it a class culture, but not specifically a bourgeois one. If this is so, we have reason to assume that the cultural revolution aims far beyond bourgeois culture, that it is directed against the aesthetic form as such, against art as such, literature as literature. And, indeed, the arguments advanced by the cultural revolution corroborate this assumption.

II

What are the main counts in the indictment of the aesthetic form?

—it is not adequately expressive of the real human condition;

—it is divorced from reality inasmuch as it creates a world of beautiful illusion (*schöner Schein*), of poetic justice, of artistic harmony and order which reconciles the irreconcilable, justifies the unjustifiable;

—in this world of illusory reconciliation, the energy of the life instincts, the sensuous energy of the body, the creativity of matter which are forces of liberation are repressed; and, by virtue of these features,

—the aesthetic form is a factor of stabilization in the repressive society and thus is itself repressive.

At one of the early manifestations of the cultural revolution, at the first surrealist exposition in London, Herbert Read programmatically formulated this relation between classical art and repression:

Classicism, let it be stated without further preface, represents for us now, and has always represented, the forces of oppression. Classicism is the intellectual counterpart of political tyranny. It was so in the ancient world and in the medieval empires; it was renewed to express the dictatorships of the Renaissance and has ever since been the official creed of capitalism.

[And later] The norms of classical art are the typical patterns of order, proportion, symmetry, equilibruim, harmony and of all static and inorganic qualities. They are intellectual concepts which control or repress the vital instincts on which growth and therefore change depend, and in no sense represent a freely determined preference, but merely an imposed ideal.*

Today's cultural revolution extends Herbert Read's rejection of Classicism to practically all styles, to the very essence of bourgeois art.

At stake is the "affirmative character" of bourgeois culture, by virtue of which art serves to beautify and justify the established order.** The aesthetic form responds to the misery of the isolated bourgeois individual by celebrating universal humanity, to physical deprivation by exalting the beauty of the soul, to external servitude by elevating the value of inner freedom.

But this affirmation has its own dialectic. There is no work of art which does not break its affirmative stance by the "power of the negative," which does not, in its very structure, evoke the words, the images, the music of another reality, of another order repelled by the existing one and yet alive in memory and anticipation, alive in what happens to men and women, and in their rebellion against it. Where this tension between affirmation and negation, between pleasure and sorrow, higher and

* *Surrealism,* edited with an introduction by Herbert Read (New York: Harcourt, Brace and Co., 1936), pp. 23, 25 f.
** See my article *Der affirmative Charakter der Kultur* (1937), English translation in *Negations* (Boston: Beacon Press, 1968), pp. 88 ff., especially p. 98.

material culture no longer prevails, where the work no longer sustains the dialectical unity of what is and what can (and ought to) be, art has lost its truth, has lost itself. And precisely in the aesthetic form are this tension, and the critical, negating, transcending qualities of bourgeois art—its antibourgeois qualities. To recapture and transform them, to save them from expulsion must be one of the tasks of the cultural revolution.

This different, positive evaluation of the aesthetic form, its validation for the radical reconstruction of society, seems to be called for by the new stage of the historical process in which the cultural revolution is placed: the stage of the intensified disintegration of the capitalist system, and of the intensified reaction against it, namely, the counterrevolutionary organization of suppression. To the degree to which the latter prevails over the former, to that degree the opposition is "displaced" to the cultural and subcultural realm, to find there the images and tones which may break through the established universe of discourse and preserve the future.

The situation is worse now than it was in the period from the beginning of modern art (in the last third of the 19th century) to the ascent of fascism. The revolution in the West was defeated, fascism has shown a way to institutionalize terror in order to save the capitalist system, and in the most advanced industrial country which still dominates this system on a global scale, the working class is not a revolutionary class. Though the classical bourgeois culture is no more, the development of an independent post-bourgeois (socialist) culture has been arrested. Without soil and basis in society, the cultural revolution appears as the abstract negation rather than the historical heir of bourgeois culture. Not carried by a revolutionary class, it seeks support in two different, and even contrary, directions; on the one side, it tries to give word, image, and tone to the feelings and needs of "the masses" (which are not revolutionary); on the other side, it elaborates anti-forms which are constituted by the mere atomization and fragmentation of traditional forms: poems which are simply ordinary prose cut up in verse lines, paintings which substitute a merely technical arrangement of parts and pieces for any meaningful whole, music which replaces the highly "intellectual," "other-worldly" classical harmony by a highly spontaneous, open polyphony. But the anti-forms are incapable of bridging the gap between "real life" and art. And against these tendencies stand those which, while radically revamping the bourgeois tradition, preserve its progressive qualities.

In this tradition, order, proportion, harmony have indeed been essential aesthetic qualities. However, these qualities are neither "intellectual concepts," nor do they represent the "forces of repression." They are rather the opposite: the idea, ideation of a redeemed, liberated world—freed from the forces of repression. These qualities are "static" because the *oeuvre* "binds" the destructive movement of reality, because it has a perpetual "end," * but: This is the static of fulfillment, of rest: *the end of violence;* the ever-renewed hope which closes the tragedies of Shakespeare—the hope that the world may now be different. It is the static quality in the music of Orpheus which arrests the struggle of the animal existence—perhaps a quality in all great music.** The norms governing the order of

* This raises the question whether art does not in itself contain a limitation of subject matter; whether certain subjects are not a priori excluded as incompatible with art. For example, the presentation—without the negating qualities—of cruelty, violence, et cetera. There certainly are great paintings of battle scenes, torture, the crucifixion which do not invoke the rebellion against that which happens. Are they really works of art in a more than purely technical sense, and therefore without that message of truth which is art's own truth? Then indeed, art becomes wholly affirmative; even the most perfect aesthetic qualities do not save the work from becoming a "decoration"; it lacks (inner) necessity.

** Nietzsche asked, "Does perhaps music pertain to a culture where the dominion of all kinds of violence (*Gewaltmenschen*) has already come to an end?" *Werke* (Stuttgart: Alfred Kröner), vol. XVI, 1911, p. 260.

art are not those governing reality but rather norms of its *negation:* it is the order which would prevail in the land of Mignon, of Baudelaire's *Invitation au Voyage,* of the landscapes of Claude Lorrain . . . ; the order which obeys the "laws of beauty," of *form.*

To be sure, the aesthetic form contains *another order* which may indeed represent the forces of oppression, namely, that which subjects man and things to the *raison d'état,* or to the reason of the established society. This is an order which demands resignation, authority, control of "the vital instincts," recognition of the right of that which is. And this order is enforced by Fate, or the gods, kings, wise men, or by conscience and guilt feeling, or it is just there. It is the order which triumphs over Hamlet, Lear, Shylock, Antony, Berenice and Phèdre, Mignon, Madame Bovary, Julien Sorel, Romeo and Juliet, Don Juan, Violetta—over the dissenters, victims, and lovers of all times. But even where the impartial justice of the *oeuvre* all but absolves the power of reality from the crime of oppression, the aesthetic form denies this impartiality and exalts the victim: the truth is in the beauty, tenderness, and passion of the victims, and not in the rationality of the oppressors.

The norms which govern the aesthetic order are *not* "intellectual concepts." To be sure, there is no authentic *oeuvre* without the utmost intellectual effort and intellectual discipline in the formation of the material. There is no such thing as "automatic" art, nor does art "imitate": it comprehends the world. The sensuous immediacy which art attains *presupposes* a synthesis of experience according to universal principles, which alone can lend to the *oeuvre* more than private significance. This is the synthesis of two antagonistic levels of reality: the established order of things, and the possible or impossible liberation from it—on both levels, interplay between the historical and the universal. In the synthesis itself, sensibility, imagination, and understanding are joined.

The result is the creation of an object world other than and yet derived from the existing one, but this transformation does not do violence to the objects (man and things)—it rather speaks for them, gives word and tone and image to that which is silent, distorted, suppressed in the established reality. And this liberating and cognitive power, inherent in art, is in all its styles and forms. Even in the realistic novel or painting, which tells a story the way it could indeed happen (and perhaps did happen) at that time and place, the story is changed by the aesthetic form. In the *oeuvre*, men and women may talk and act the way they did "in reality"; things may look as they do "in reality"—still, another dimension is present: in the description of the environment, the structuring of (inner and outer) time and space, in the marked silence, in that which is not there,* and in the microcosmic (or macrocosmic) view of things. Thus, we can say that, in the aesthetic order, things are moved into their place which is *not* the place they "happen to have," and that, in this transformation, they come into their own.

To be sure, the aesthetic transformation is *imaginary*— it must be imaginary, for what faculty other than the imagination could invoke the sensuous presence of that which is *not* (yet)? And this transformation is sensuous rather than conceptual; it must be enjoyable ("disinterested pleasure"); it remains committed to harmony. Does this commitment make the traditional art inevitably an agent of repression, a dimension of the respective Establishment?

---

* Merleau-Ponty with reference to Stendhal: "One can narrate the subject of a novel like that of a painting, but the force of the novel, like that of a painting, is not in the subject. What counts is not so much that Julien Sorel, when he hears that Mme. de Rènal has betrayed him, goes to Verrière and tries to kill her—what counts is, after the news, this silence, this dream cavalcade, this certainty without thought, this eternal resolution . . . But all this is nowhere said." (Maurice Merleau-Ponty, *La Prose du monde* [Paris: Gallimard, 1969], p. 124.)

III

The affirmative character of art was grounded not so much in its divorce from reality as in the ease with which it could be reconciled with the given reality, used as its décor, taught and experienced as uncommitting but rewarding value, the possession of which distinguished the "higher" order of society, the educated, from the masses. But the affirmative power of art is also the power which denies this affirmation. In spite of its (feudal and bourgeois) use as status symbol, conspicuous consumption, refinement, art retains that alienation from the established reality which is at the origin of art. It is a second alienation, by virtue of which the artist dissociates himself methodically from the alienated society and creates the unreal, "illusory" universe in which art alone has, and communicates, its truth. At the same time, this alienation *relates* art to society: it preserves the class content—and makes it transparent. As "ideology," art "invalidates" dominant ideology. The class content is "idealized," stylized, and thereby becomes the receptacle of a universal truth beyond the particular class content. Thus the classical theater stylizes the world of the real princes, nobles, burghers of the respective period. Although this ruling class hardly talked and acted like its protagonists on the stage, it could at least recognize in them its own ideology, its own ideal or model (or caricature).* The court of Versailles could still understand the theater of Corneille and recognize there its ideological code; similarly, the court of Weimar could still be expected to find its ideology in the court of Thaos in Goethe's *Iphigénie,* or in the court of Ferrara in his *Torquato Tasso.*

The medium in which art and reality met was the style of

* See Leo Lowenthal, *Literature and the Image of Man* (Boston: Beacon Press, 1957), especially the introduction and Chapter IV.

life. The parasitic nobility had its own aesthetic form which demanded a ritual behavior: honor, dignity, display of pleasure, even "higher culture," education. The classical theater was the *mimesis* and, at the same time, the critical idealization of this order. But through all accommodation, through all kinship to the established reality, the theater proclaims its own dissociation from it. The artistic alienation appears in the theater as its historical décor, its language, its "exaggerations" and condensations.

The modes of alienation change with the basic changes in society. With the capitalist democratization and industrialization, classicism has indeed lost much of its truth—it has lost its affinity, its kinship to the code and culture of the ruling class. Any affinity between the White House and classicism is beyond the stretch of even the most absurd imagination, and what was still faintly conceivable in France under de Gaulle has become inconceivable under his successor.

The artistic alienation makes the work of art, the universe of art, essentially unreal—it creates a world which does not exist, a world of *Schein*, appearance, illusion. But in this transformation of reality into illusion, and only in it, appears the subversive truth of art.

In this universe, every word, every color, every sound is "new," different—breaking the familiar context of perception and understanding, of sense certainty and reason in which men and nature are enclosed. By becoming components of the aesthetic form, words, sounds, shapes, and colors are insulated against their familiar, ordinary use and function; thus they are freed for a new dimension of existence.* This is the achieve-

---

* Here is Merleau-Ponty's magnificent description of the methodical alienation in Cézanne's paintings. Cézanne breaks with the customary experience of our world: "[il] révèle le fond de nature inhumaine sur lequel l'homme s'installe. C'est pourquoi ses personnages sont étranges et comme vus par un être d'une autre espèce. La nature elle-même est dépouillée

ment of the *style*, which *is* the poem, the novel, the painting, the composition. The style, embodiment of the aesthetic form, in subjecting reality to another order, subjects it to the "laws of beauty."

True and false, right and wrong, pain and pleasure, calm and violence become aesthetic categories within the framework of the *oeuvre*. Thus deprived of their (immediate) reality, they enter a different context in which even the ugly, cruel, sick become parts of the aesthetic harmony governing the whole. They are thereby not "canceled": the horror in Goya's etchings remains horror, but at the same time "eternalizes" the horror of horror.

IV

In Chapter 2, I referred to the subterranean survival of the ancient theory of recollection in Marxian theory. The notion aimed at a repressed quality in men and things which, once recognized, could drive toward a radical change in the relation between man and nature. The discussion of early Marxian theory traced the concept of recollection in the context of the "emancipation of the senses": "aesthetic" as pertaining to sensibility. Now, in discussing the critical theory of art, the notion of recollection is again suggested: "aesthetic" as pertaining to art.

On a primary level, art is recollection: it appeals to a preconceptual experience and understanding which reemerge in and against the context of the social functioning of experience and understanding—against instrumentalist reason and sensibility.

des attributs qui la préparent pour des communions animistes: le paysage est sans vent, l'eau du lac d'Annecy sans mouvement, les objets gelés hésitants comme à l'origine de la terre. C'est un monde sans familiarité, où l'on n'est pas bien, qui interdit toute effusion humaine." ("Le Doute de Cézanne," in *Sens et Non-Sens* [Paris: Nagel, 1948], p. 30.)

When it attains this primary level—the terminal point of the intellectual effort—art violates taboos: it lends voice and sight and ear to things which are normally repressed: dreams, memories, longings—ultimate states of sensibility. Here is no more superimposed restraint: the form, far from repressing the full content, makes it appear in its integrity. Here is also no more conformity and no more rebellion—only sorrow and joy. These extreme qualities, the supreme points of art, seem to be the prerogative of music (which "gives the innermost kernel preceding all form, or the heart of things"),* and within music, of melody. Here the melody—dominant, *cantabile*, is the basic unit of recollection: recurring through all variations, remaining when it is cut off and no longer carries the composition, it sustains the supreme point: in and against the richness and complexity of the work. It is the voice, beauty, calm of another world here on earth, and it is mainly this voice which constitutes the two-dimensional structure of classical and romantic music.

In the classical theater, the verse is the dominant voice of the two-dimensional world. The verse challenges the rule of ordinary language and becomes a vehicle for the expression of that which remains unsaid in the established reality. Again, it is the rhythm of the verse which renders possible, prior to all specific content, the eruption of the unreal reality and its truth. The "laws of beauty" form reality in order to make it transparent. It is the "sublimated" mode in which the protagonists of the classical theater speak, and not only what they do and suffer, which evokes and at the same time rejects that which is.

The bourgeois theater (meaning here: the theater in which the protagonists are members of the bourgeoisie) moves from the beginning in a desublimated, de-idealized, aesthetic universe. Prose replaces verse; the historic décor is dropped;

* Arthur Schopenhauer, *The World As Will and Representation*, translated by E. F. J. Payne (New York: Dover), I, § 52.

realism prevails. The classical form gives way to open forms ("Storm and Stress"). But the egalitarian ideas of the bourgeois revolution explode the realistic universe: the class conflict between nobility and bourgeoisie assumes the form of a tragedy for which there is no solution. And when this class conflict no longer holds the center of the stage, the specific bourgeois content is transcended: the bourgeois world is shattered by symbolic figures or configurations which become the messengers of catastrophe and liberation (Ibsen, Gerhart Hauptmann).

The novel is not closed to this aesthetic transcendence. No matter which particular "plot" or environment is the subject matter of the novel, its prose can shatter the established universe. Kafka is perhaps the most outstanding example. From the beginning, the links with the given reality are cut by calling things by their names, which turn out to be misnomers. The discrepancy between that which the name says and that which *is* becomes unconquerable. Or is it rather the coincidence, the literal identity between the two, which is the horror? In any case, this language breaks through the masquerade: the illusion is in the reality itself—not in the work of art. This work is in its very structure rebellion—with the world it depicts, there is no conceivable reconciliation.

It is this second alienation which disappears in today's systematic efforts to reduce, if not close, the gap between art and reality. The effort is doomed to failure. Certainly, there is rebellion in the guerrilla theater, in the poetry of the "free press," in rock music—but it remains artistic without the negating power of art. To the degree to which it makes itself part of real life, it loses the transcendence which opposes art to the established order—it remains *immanent* in this order, one-dimensional, and thus succumbs to this order. Precisely its immediate "life quality" is the undoing of this anti-art, and of its appeal. It *moves* (literally and figuratively) here and now, within the existing universe, and it terminates in the frustrated outcry for its abrogation.

There is indeed a profound uneasiness toward classical and romantic art. Somehow, it seems a thing of the past: it seems to have lost its truth, its meaning. Is it because this art is too sublime, because it substitutes for the real, living soul an "intellectual," metaphysical soul, and is therefore repressive? Or could it be *the other way around?*

Perhaps the extreme qualities of this art strike us today as an all too *un*sublimated, direct, unrestrained expression of passion and pain—some sort of shame reacts against this kind of exhibitionism and "outpouring" of the soul. Perhaps we can no longer cope with this *pathos* which drives to the limits of the human existence—and beyond the limits of social restraint. Perhaps this art presupposes, on the part of the recipient, that distance of reflection and contemplation, that self-chosen silence and receptivity which today's "living art" rejects.

The atrophy of the organs for artistic alienation is the result of very material processes. The totalitarian organization of society, its violence and aggressiveness have invaded the inner and outer space where the extreme aesthetic qualities of art can still be experienced and accepted with good faith. They contradict too blatantly the horrors of reality, and this contradiction appears as escape from a reality from which there is no escape. They require a degree of emancipation from immediate experience, of "privacy," which has become all but impossible, false. This is non-behavioral, non-operational art: it does not "activate" to anything but reflection and remembrance—the promise of the dream. But the dream must become a force of changing rather than dreaming the human condition: it must become a political force. If art dreams of liberation within the spectrum of history, dream realization through revolution must be possible—the surrealist program must still be valid. Does the cultural revolution testify to this possibility?

V

The cultural revolution remains a radically progressive force. However, in its efforts to free the political potential of art, it is blocked by an *unsolved contradiction*. A subversive potential is in the very nature of art—but how can it be translated into reality today, that is to say, how can it be expressed so that it can become a guide and element in the *praxis* of change without ceasing to be art, without losing its *internal* subversive force? How can it be translated in such a manner that the aesthetic form is replaced by "something *real*," alive, and yet *transcending* and *denying* the established reality?

Art can express its radical potential only *as art*, in its own language and image, which *invalidate* the ordinary language, the *"prose du monde."* The liberating "message" of art also *transcends* the actually attainable goals of liberation, just as it transcends the actual critique of society. Art remains committed to the Idea (Schopenhauer), to the universal in the particular; and since the tension between idea and reality, between the universal and the particular, is likely to persist until the millennium which will never be, art must remain *alienation*. If art, because of this alienation, does not "speak" to the masses, this is the work of the class society which creates and perpetuates the masses. If and when a classless society achieves the transformation of the masses into "freely associated" individuals, art would have lost its elitist character, but not its estrangement from society. The tension between affirmation and negation precludes any identification of art with revolutionary *praxis*. Art cannot represent the revolution,* it can only

* Certainly, there are the great presentations of the French Revolution in Büchner's *Dantons Tod*, of 1848 in Flaubert's *Education Sentimentale*—they are critical, if not hostile presentations, hostile to the actual revolutionary practice and its exigencies. There is William Blake's

invoke it in another medium, in an aesthetic form in which the political content becomes *meta*political, governed by the internal necessity of art. And the goal of all revolution—a world of tranquillity and freedom—appears in a totally unpolitical medium, under the laws of beauty, of harmony. Thus Stravinsky heard the revolution in Beethoven's quartets:

> My further, personal belief is that the quartets are a charter of human rights, and a perpetually seditious one in the Platonic sense of the subversiveness of art . . .
> A high concept of freedom *is* embodied in the quartets, . . . both beyond and including what Beethoven himself meant when he wrote [to Prince Galitzin] that his music could "help suffering mankind." They are a measure of man . . . and part of the description of the quality of man, and their existence is a guarantee.*

There is a symbolic event which announces the transition from everyday life to an essentially different medium, the "leap" from the established social universe to the estranged universe of art; this is the occurrence of *silence:*

> The moment at which a piece of music begins provides a clue to the nature of all art. The incongruity of that moment, compared to the uncounted, unperceived silence which preceded it, is the secret of art . . . it is in the distinction between the actual

---

magnificent epic fragment—which ends prior to the meeting of the Etats Généraux: the fragment is a cosmic transfiguration of the revolution, where mountains, valleys, and streams join the political struggle.

* Igor Stravinsky, in *The New York Review of Books*, April 24, 1969, p. 4.

and the desirable. All art is an attempt to define and
make unnatural this distinction.*

And this silence becomes part of the aesthetic form not only in
music: it permeates the entire work of Kafka; it is ever present
in Beckett's *End Game*; it is in a painting of Cézanne.

> . . . [the painter's] only aspiration must be to si-
> lence. He must stifle within himself the voices of prej-
> udice, he must forget, and keep on forgetting, he must
> make silence all about him, he must be a perfect
> echo.**

An "echo" not of what is immediate nature, reality, but of
that reality which erupts in the artist's estrangement from the
immediate reality—even from that of the revolution.

The relation between art and revolution is a unity of opposites, an antagonistic unity. Art obeys a necessity, and has a
freedom which is its own—not those of the revolution. Art and
revolution are united in "changing the world"—liberation. But
in its practice, art does not abandon its own exigencies and does
not quit its own dimension: it remains non-operational. In art,
the political goal appears only in the transfiguration which is
the aesthetic form. The revolution may well be absent from the
oeuvre even while the artist himself is "engaged," is a revolutionary.

André Breton recalls the case of Courbet and Rimbaud.
During the Commune of 1871, Courbet was a member of the
Council of the Commune, he was held responsible for the dis-

---

* John Berger, *The Moment of Cubism* (New York: Pantheon,
1969), pp. 31 f.
** Cézanne, as quoted by Gasquet in Max Raphael, *The Demands
of Art*, translation by Norbert Guterman, Bolingen Series LXXVIII
(Princeton: Princeton University Press, 1968), p. 8.

mantling of the Vendôme column. He fought for a "free and nonprivileged" art. Yet there is no direct testimony of the revolution in his paintings (although there is in his drawings); there is no political content. After the collapse of the Commune, and after the massacre of its heroes, Courbet paints still lifes.

> . . . some of these apples . . . , prodigious, colossal, extraordinary in their weight and sensuality, are more powerful and more "protestaire" than any political painting.*

Breton writes:

> Everything happens as if he had decided that there must be some way to reflect his profound faith in the betterment of the world in everything that he tried to evoke, some way to make it appear somehow in the light he caused to fall on the horizon or on a roebuck's belly.**

And Rimbaud: he sympathized with the Commune; he drafted a constitution for a communist society, but the tenor of his poems written under the immediate impact of the Commune "in no way differs from that of the other poems." The revolution was in his poetry from the beginning and to the end: as a preoccupation of a technical order, namely, to translate the world into a new language.†

The political "engagement" becomes a problem of artistic

---

* André Fernigier, quoted in Robert Fernier, *Gustave Courbet* (Paris: Bibliothèque des Arts, 1969), p. 110.
** *Manifestos of Surrealism*, translation by R. Scaver and Helen R. Lane (Ann Arbor: University of Michigan Press, 1969), p. 219.
† *Ibid.*, p. 220.

"technique," and instead of translating art (poetry) into reality, reality is translated into a new aesthetic form. The radical refusal, the protest, appears in the way in which words are grouped and regrouped, freed from their familiar use and abuse. *Alchemy of the word;* the image, the sound, creation of another reality out of the existing one—permanent imaginary revolution, emergence of a "second history" within the historical continuum.

Permanent aesthetic subversion—this is the way of art.

The abolition of the aesthetic form, the notion that art could become a component part of revolutionary (and prerevolutionary) *praxis,* until under fully developed socialism, it would be adequately translated into reality (or absorbed by "science")—this notion is false and oppressive: it would mean the end of art. Martin Walser has well formulated this falsehood with respect to literature:

> The metaphor of the "death of literature" comes an eternity too early: Only when the objects and their names would melt into one (*in eins verschmelzen*), only then would literature be dead. As long as this paradisical state has not arrived, the struggle for the objects (*Streit um die Gegenstände*) will also be waged with the help of words.*

And the meaning of the words will continue to devaluate their ordinary meaning: they (as well as the images and tones) will continue the imaginary transformation of the object world, man, and nature. Coincidence of words and things: this would mean that all the potentialities of things would be realized, that the "power of the negative" would have ceased to operate —it would mean that the imagination has become wholly functional: servant to instrumentalist Reason.

* In *Kursbuch* 20, March 1970 (Frankfurt: Suhrkamp), p. 37.

I have spoken of "art as a form of reality" * in a free society. The phrase is ambiguous. It was supposed to indicate an essential aspect of liberation, namely, the radical transformation of the technical and natural universe in accordance with the emancipated sensibility (and rationality) of man. I still hold this view. But the goal is a permanent one; that is to say, no matter in what form, art can never eliminate the tension between art and reality. Elimination of this tension would be the impossible final unity of subject and object: the materialistic version of absolute idealism. It denies the insurmountable limit to the mutability of human nature: a biological, not theological, limit. To interpret this irredeemable alienation of art as a mark of bourgeois (or any other) class society is nonsense.

The nonsense has a basis in fact. The aesthetic representation of the Idea, of the universal in the particular, leads art to transform particular (historical) conditions into universal ones: to show as the tragic or cosmic fate of man what is only his fate in the established society. There is, in the Western tradition, the celebration of an unnecessary tragedy, an unnecessary fate—unnecessary to the extent to which they pertain, not to *the* human condition but rather to specific social institutions and ideologies. I have previously referred to a work in which the class content seems most conspicuously the substance: the catastrophe of *Madame Bovary* is evidently due to the specific situation of the petty bourgeoisie in a French province. Nevertheless, you can, in your imagination, in reading the story, remove (or rather "bracket") the "external," extraneous environment, and you will read, in the story, the refusal and denial of the world of the French petty bourgeois, their values, their morality, their aspirations and desires, namely, the fate of

* In *On the Future of Art*, essays by Arnold J. Toynbee, Louis I. Kahn, and others, edited by Edward Fry (New York: Viking Press, 1970), pp. 123 ff.

men and women caught in the catastrophe of love. Enlighten-
ment, democracy, and psychoanalysis may mitigate the typically feudal or bourgeois conflicts and perhaps even change the
outcome—the tragic substance would remain. This interplay
between the universal and the particular, between class content and transcending form *is* the history of art.

Perhaps there is a "scale" according to which the class
content appears most distinctly in literature and least distinctly
(if at all!) in music (Schopenhauer's hierarchy of the arts!).
The *word* communicates daily the society to its members; it becomes a name for the objects as they are made, shaped, used
by the established society. Colors, shapes, tones do not carry
such "meaning": they are in a sense more universal, "neutral"
toward their social usage. In contrast, the word can all but *lose*
its transcendent meaning—and tends to do so the more society
approaches the stage of total control over the universe of discourse. Then we can indeed speak of a "coincidence between
the name and its object"—but a false, enforced, deceptive coincidence: instrument of domination.

I refer again to the use of Orwellian language as normal
means of communication. The rule of this language over the
minds and bodies of men is more than outright brainwashing,
more than the systematic application of lies as means of manipulation. In a sense, this language is correct; it expresses, quite
innocently, the omnipresent contradictions which permeate
this society. Under the regime it has given itself, striving for
peace is indeed waging war (against the "communists" everywhere); ending the war means exactly what the warfaring government is doing—though it may in fact be the opposite,
namely, intensifying rather than extending the slaughter;*
freedom is exactly that which the people have under the Administration—though it may in fact be the opposite; tear gas

---

* See the Cornell report on intensified bombing in Indochina, *New
York Times,* November 6, 1971.

and plant killers are indeed "legitimate and humane" against the Vietnamese for they cause "less suffering" to the people than "burning them to death with napalm" *—apparently the only alternative open to this government. These blatant contradictions may well enter the consciousness of the people—this does not change the fact that the word *as defined* by the (public or private) administration remains valid, effective, operational: it stimulates the desired behavior and action. Language assumes again magical character: a government spokesman has only to pronounce the words "national security" and he gets what he wants—rather sooner than later.

VI

At precisely this stage, the radical effort to sustain and intensify the "power of the negative," the subversive potential of art, must sustain and intensify the *alienating* power of art: the aesthetic form, in which alone the radical force of art becomes communicable.

In his essay *"Die Phantasie im Spätkapitalismus und die Kulturrevolution,"* Peter Schneider calls this recapture of the aesthetic transcendence the "propagandistic function of art":

> Propagandistic art would seek in the recorded dream history (*Wunschgeschichte*) of mankind the utopian images, would free them from the distorted forms which were imposed upon them by the material conditions of life, and show to these dreams (*Wünschen*) the road to realization which now, finally, has become possible. . . . The aesthetic of this art should be the strategy of dream realization.**

* *Kursbuch* 16, 1969, p. 31.
** G. Warren Nutter, Assistant Secretary of Defense for International Security, *New York Times*, March 23, 1971.

This strategy of realization, precisely because it is to be that of a dream, can never be "complete," never be a translation into reality, which would make art into a psychoanalytic process. Realization rather means finding the *aesthetic* forms which can communicate the possibilities of a liberating transformation of the technical and natural environment. But here, too, the distance between art and practice, the dissociation of the former from the latter, remain.

At the time between the two World Wars, where the protest seemed to be directly translatable into action, joined to action, where the shattering of the aesthetic form seemed to be the response to the revolutionary forces in action, Antonin Artaud formulated the program for the abolition of art: *"En finir avec les chefs-d'oeuvres"*: art must become the concern of the masses (la foule), must be an affair of the streets, and above all, of the organism, the body, of nature. Thus, it would *move* men, would move things, for: "il faut que les choses crèvent pour repartir et recommencer." The serpent moves to the tones of the music not because of their "spiritual content" but because their vibrations communicate themselves through the earth to the serpent's entire body. Art has cut off this communication and "deprived a gesture (*un geste*) from its repercussion in the organism": this unity with nature must be restored: "beneath the poetry of text, there is a poetry *tout court*, without form and without text." This natural poetry must be recaptured which is still present in the eternal myths of mankind (such as "beneath the text" in Sophocles' *Oedipus*) and in the magic of the primitives: its rediscovery is prerequisite for the liberation of man. For "we are not free, and the sky can still fall on our head. And the theater is made first of all in order to teach us all this." * To attain this goal, the theater must leave

* Antonin Artaud, *Le Théâtre et son double* (Paris: Gallimard, 1964), pp. 113, 124, 123, 119, 121 (written in 1933).

the stage and go on the street, to the masses. And it must
shock, cruelly shock and *shatter* the complacent consciousness
and unconscious.

> [a theater] where violent physical images crush
> and hypnotize the sensibility of the spectator, seized
> in the theater as by a whirlwind of superior forces.*

Even at the time when Artaud wrote, the "superior forces"
were of a very different kind, and they seized man, not to liberate but rather to enslave and destroy him more effectively. And
today, what possible language, what possible image can crush
and hypnotize minds and bodies which live in peaceful coexist-
ence (and even profiting from) genocide, torture, and
poison? ** And if Artaud wants a "constant sonorization":
sounds and noises and cries, first for their quality of vibration
and then for that which they represent," † we ask: has not the
audience, even the "natural" audience on the streets, long since
become familiar with the violent noises, cries, which are the
daily equipment of the mass media, sports, highways, places
of recreation? They do not break the oppressive familiarity with
destruction; they reproduce it.

    The German writer Peter Handke blasted the *"ekelhafte
Unwahrheit von Ernsthaftigkeiten im Spielraum* (the loath-
some untruth of seriousness in play)." ‡ This indictment is
not an attempt to keep politics out of the theater, but to indicate the form in which it can find expression. The indictment
cannot be upheld with respect to Greek tragedy, to Shakespeare,
Racine, Kleist, Ibsen, Brecht, Beckett: there, by virtue of the

* *Ibid.,* p. 126.
** *Ibid.*
† *Ibid.,* p. 124.
‡ Quoted in Yark Karsunke, "Die Strasse und das Theater," in
Kursbuch 20, *loc. cit.,* p. 67.

aesthetic form, the "play" creates its own universe of "serious-ness" which is *not* that of the given reality, but rather its nega-tion. But the indictment holds for the guerrilla theater of today: it is a *contradictio in adjecto;* altogether different from the Chi-nese (whether played on or after the Long March); there, the theater did not take place in a "universe of play"; it was part of a revolution in actual process, and established, as an episode, the identity between the players and the fighters: unity of the space of the play and the space of the revolution.

The Living Theatre may serve as an example of self-defeat-ing purpose.* It makes a systematic attempt to unite the theater and the Revolution, the play and the battle, bodily and spiritual liberation, individual internal and social external change. But this union is shrouded in mysticism: "the Kabbalah, Tantric and Hasidic teaching, the I Ching, and other sources." The mix-ture of Marxism and mysticism, of Lenin and Dr. R. D. Laing does not work; it vitiates the political impulse. The liberation of the body, the sexual revolution, becoming a ritual to be per-formed ("the rite of universal intercourse"), loses its place in the political revolution: if sex is a voyage to God, it can be tolerated even in extreme forms. The revolution of love, the nonviolent revolution, is no serious threat; the powers that be have always been capable of coping with the forces of love. The radical desublimation which takes place in the theater, *as* theater, is organized, arranged, performed desublimation—it is close to turning into its opposite.**

* See *Paradise Now,* Collective Creation of the Living Theatre, written down by Judith Melina and Julian Beck (New York: Random House, 1971).

** In the summer of 1971, the Living Theater group that had been playing before the wretched of the earth in Brazil was incarcerated by the fascist government. There, in the midst of the terror which is the life of the people, and which precluded any integration into the established order; even the mystified liberation play seemed a threat to the regime. I wish to express my solidarity with Judith Malina and Julian Beck and their group; my criticism is fraternal, since we share the same struggle.

Untruth is the fate of the unsublimated, direct representation. Here, the "illusory" character of art is not abolished but doubled: the players only play the actions they want to demonstrate, and this action itself is unreal, is play.

The distinction between an internal revolution of the aesthetic form and its destruction, between authentic and contrived directness (a distinction based on the tension between art and reality), has also become decisive in the development (and function) of "living music," "natural music." It is as if the cultural revolution had fulfilled Artaud's demand that, in a literal sense, music move the body, thereby drawing nature into the rebellion. Life music has indeed an authentic basis: *black music* as the cry and song of the slaves and the ghettos.°
In this music, the very life and death of black men and women are lived again: the music *is* body; the aesthetic form is the "gesture" of pain, sorrow, indictment. With the takeover by the whites, a significant change occurs: white "rock" is what its black paradigm is *not,* namely, *performance.* It is as if the

___

° Pierre Lere analyzes the dialectic of this black music in his article "Free Jazz: Évolution ou Révolution":
". . . the liberty of the musical forms is only the aesthetic translation of the will to social liberation. Transcending the tonal framework of the theme, the musician finds himself in a position of freedom. This search for freedom is translated into atonal musicality; it defines a modal climate where the Black expresses a new order. The melodic line becomes the medium of communication between an initial order which is rejected and a final order which is hoped for. The frustrating possession of the one, joined with the liberating attainment of the other, establishes a rupture in between the Weft of harmony which gives way to an aesthetic of the cry (*esthétique du cri*). This cry, the characteristic resonant (*sonore*) element of "free music," born in an exasperated tension, announces the violent rupture with the established white order and translates the advancing (*promotrice*) violence of a new black order." (*Revue d'Esthétique,* vols. 3–4, 1970, pp. 320, 321.)

crying and shouting, the jumping and playing, now take place
in an artificial, organized space; that they are directed toward
a (sympathetic) *audience*. What had been part of the perma-
nence of life, now becomes a concert, a festival, a disc in the
making. "The group" becomes a fixed entity (*verdinglicht*),
absorbing the individuals; it is "totalitarian" in the way in
which it overwhelms individual consciousness and mobilizes a
collective unconscious which remains without social foundation.

And as this music loses its radical impact, it tends to mas-
sification: the listeners and co-performers in the audience are
masses streaming to a spectacle, a performance.

True, in this spectacle, the audience actively participates:
the music *moves* their bodies, makes them "natural." But their
(literally) electrical excitation often assumes the features of
hysteria. The aggressive force of the endlessly repeated ham-
mering rhythm (the variations of which do not open another
dimension of music), the squeezing dissonances, the standardized "frozen" distortions, the noise level in general—is it
not the force of frustration?* And the identical gestures, the
twisting and shaking of bodies which rarely (if ever) really
touch each other—it seems like treading on the spot, it does
not get you anywhere except into a mass soon to disperse. This
music is, in a literal sense, *imitation, mimesis* of effective
aggression: it is, moreover, another case of *catharsis:* group
therapy which, temporarily, removes inhibitions. Liberation remains a private affair.

* The frustration behind the noisy aggression is revealed very
neatly in a statement by Grace Slick of the "Jefferson Airplane"
group, reported in the *New York Times Magazine* (October 18, 1970):
"Our eternal goal in life, Grace says, absolutely deadpan, is to get
louder."

The tension between art and revolution seems irreducible. Art itself, in practice, cannot change reality, and art cannot submit to the actual requirements of the revolution without denying itself. But art can and will draw its inspirations, and its very form, from the then-prevailing revolutionary movement—for revolution is in the substance of art. The historical substance of art asserts itself in all modes of alienation; it precludes any notion that recapturing the aesthetic form today could mean revival of classicism, romanticism, or any other traditional form. Does an analysis of the social reality allow any indication as to art forms which would respond to the revolutionary potential in the contemporary world?

According to Adorno, art responds to the total character of repression and administration with total alienation. The highly intellectual, constructivist, and at the same time spontaneous-formless music of John Cage, Stockhausen, Pierre Boulez may be the extreme examples.

But has this effort already reached the point of no return, that is, the point where the *oeuvre* drops out of the dimension of alienation, of *formed* negation and contradiction, and turns into a sound-game, language-game—harmless and without commitment, shock which no longer shocks, and thus succumbing?

The radical literature which speaks in formless semi-spontaneity and directness loses with the aesthetic form the political content, while this content erupts in the most highly formed poems of Allan Ginsberg and Ferlinghetti. The most uncompromising, most extreme indictment has found expression in a work which precisely because of its radicalism repels the political sphere: in the work of Samuel Beckett, there is no hope which can be translated into political terms, the aesthetic form excludes all accommodation and leaves literature as literature. And as literature, the work carries one single message: to make an end with things as they are. Similarly, the revolution is in Bertolt Brecht's most perfect lyric rather than in his political plays, and in Alban Berg's *Wozzeck* rather than in today's anti-fascist opera.

This is the passing of anti-art, the reemergence of form. And with it we find a new expression of the inherently subversive qualities of the aesthetic dimension, especially beauty as the sensuous appearance of the idea of freedom. The delight of beauty and the horror of politics; Brecht has condensed it in five lines:

Within me there is a struggle between
The delight about the blooming apple tree
And the horror about a Hitler speech.
But only the latter
Forces me to my desk

(Translation: Reinhard Lettau)

The image of the tree remains present in the poem which is "enforced" by a Hitler speech. The horror of that which is, marks the moment of creation, is the origin of the poem which celebrates the beauty of the blooming apple tree. The political dimension remains committed to the other, the aesthetic dimension, which, in turn, assumes political value. This happens not only in the work of Brecht (who is already considered a "classic") but also in some of the radical songs of protest of today—or yesterday, especially in the lyrics and music of Bob Dylan. Beauty returns, the "soul" returns: not the one in food and "on ice" but the old and repressed one, the one that was in the *Lied,* in the melody: *cantabile.* It becomes the form of the subversive content, not as artificial revival, but as a "return of the repressed." The music, in its own development, carries the song to the point of rebellion where the voice, in word and pitch, *halts* the melody, the song, and turns into outcry, shout.

Junction of art and revolution in the aesthetic dimension,* in art itself. Art which has become capable of being political even in the (apparently) total absence of political content, where nothing remains but the poem—about what? Brecht accomplishes the miracle of making the simplest ordinary language say the unutterable: the poem invokes, for a vanishing moment, the images of a liberated world, liberated nature:

DIE LIEBENDEN

Sieh jene Kraniche in grossem Bogen!
Die Wolken, welche ihnen beigegeben
Zogen mit ihnen schon, als sie entflogen
Aus einem Leben in ein andres Leben.
In gleicher Höhe und mit gleicher Eile
Scheinen sie alle beide nur daneben.
Dass so der Kranich mit der Wolke teile
Den schönen Himmel, den sie kurz befliegen
Dass also keiner länger hier verweile
Und keines andres sehe als das Wiegen

* One only has to read some of the authentic-sounding poems of young activists (or former activists) in order to see how poetry, remaining poetry, can be political also today. These love poems are political as love poems: not where they are fashionably desublimated, verbal release of sexuality, but on the contrary: where the erotic energy finds sublimated, poetic expression—a poetic language becoming the outcry against that which is done to men and women who love in this society. In contrast, the union of love and subversion, the social liberation inherent in Eros is lost where the poetic language is abandoned in favor of versified (or pseudoversified) pig language. There is such a thing as pornography, namely, the sexual publicity, propaganda with the exhibitionist, marketable Eros. Today, the pig language and the glossy photography of sex have exchange value—not the romantic love poem.

Des andern in dem Wind, den beide spüren
Die jetzt im Fluge beieinander liegen
So mag der Wind sie in das Nichts entführen
Wenn sie nur nicht vergehen und sich bleiben
So lange kann sie beide nichts berühren
So lange kann man sie von jedem Ort vertreiben
Wo Regen drohen oder Schüsse schallen.
So under Sonn und Monds wenig verschiedenen
    Scheiben
Fliegen sie hin, einander ganz verfallen.
Wohin, ihr?—Nirgend hin.—Von wem davon?—
    Von allen.
Ihr fragt, wie lange sind sie schon beisammen?
Seit kurzem.—Und wann werden sie sich trennen?
    —Bald.
So scheint die Liebe Liebenden ein Halt.*

THE LOVERS

See those cranes in their wide sweep!
See the clouds given to be at their side
Traveling with them already when they left
One life to fly into another life.
At the same height and with the same speed
Both seem merely at each other's side.
That the crane may share with the cloud
The beautiful sky through which they briefly fly
That neither may linger here longer
And neither see but the swinging
Of the other in the wind which both feel
Now lying next to each other in flight.

* *Gedichte,* vol. II (Frankfurt: Suhrkamp, 1960), p. 210. Erich
Kahler and Theodor W. Adorno have revealed the significance of this
poem. See Adorno, *Aesthetische Theorie, loc. cit.,* p. 123.

If only they not perish and stay with each other
The wind may lead them into nothingness
They can be driven from each place
Where rain threatens and shots ring out
Nothing can touch either of them.
Thus under the sun's and the moon's little varying
    orbs
They fly on together lost and belonging to each other.
Where to, you?—Nowhere. Away from whom?—From
    all.
You ask how long are they together?
A short time. And when will they leave each other?
    Soon.
Thus seem the lovers draw strength from love.

                      (*Translation by Inge S. Marcuse*)

    The image of liberation is in the flight of the cranes, through their beautiful sky, with the clouds which accompany them: sky and clouds belong to them—without mastery and domination. The image is in their ability to flee the spaces where they are threatened: the rain and the rifle shots. They are safe as long as they remain themselves, entirely with each other. The image is a vanishing one: the wind can take them into nothingness—they would still be safe: they fly from one life into another life. Time itself matters no longer: the cranes met only a short while ago, and they will leave each other soon. Space is no longer a limit: they fly nowhere, and they flee from everyone, from all. The end is illusion: love *seems* to give duration, to conquer time and space, to evade destruction. But the illusion cannot deny the reality which it invokes: the cranes *are*, in their sky, with their clouds. The end is also denial of the illusion, insistence on its reality, realization. This insistence is in the poem's language which is prose becoming verse and song in the midst of the brutality and corruption of the *Netzestadt* (Mahagonny)—in the dialogue between a whore and a bum. There is no word in this poem which is not prose. But these words are joined to sentences, or parts of sentences which say and show what ordinary language never says and shows. The apparent "protocol statements" which seem to describe things and movements in direct perception, turn into images of that which goes beyond all direct perception: the flight into the realm of freedom which is also the realm of beauty.

Strange phenomenon: beauty as a quality which is in an opera of Verdi as well as in a Bob Dylan song, in a painting of Ingres as well as Picasso, in a phrase of Flaubert as well as James Joyce, in a gesture of the Duchess of Guermantes as well as of a hippie girl! Common to all of them is the expression, against its plastic de-erotization, of beauty as negation of the commodity world and of the performances, attitudes, looks, gestures, required by it.

The aesthetic form will continue to change as the political practice succeeds (or fails) to build a better society. At the optimum, we can envisage a universe common to art and reality, but in this common universe, art would retain its transcendence. In all likelihood, people would not talk or write or compose poetry; *la prose du monde* would persist. The "end of art" is conceivable only if men are no longer capable of distinguishing between true and false, good and evil, beautiful and ugly, present and future. This would be the state of perfect barbarism at the height of civilization—and such a state is indeed a historical possibility.

Art can do nothing to prevent the ascent of barbarism—it cannot by itself keep open its own domain in and against society. For its own preservation and development, art depends on the struggle for the abolition of the social system which generates barbarism as its own potential stage: potential form of its progress. The fate of art remains linked to that of the revolution. In this sense, it is indeed an internal exigency of art which drives the artist to the streets—to fight for the Commune, for the Bolshevist revolution, for the German revolution of 1918, for the Chinese and Cuban revolutions, for all revolutions which have the historical chance of liberation. But in doing so he leaves the universe of art and enters the larger universe of which art remains an antagonistic part: that of radical practice.

VIII

Today's cultural revolution places anew on the agenda the problems of a Marxist aesthetics. In the preceding sections, I tried to make a tentative contribution to this subject; an adequate discussion would require another book. But one specific question must again be raised in this context, namely, the meaning, and the very possibility, of a "proletarian literature" (or working class literature). In my view, the discussion has never again reached the theoretical level it attained in the twenties and early thirties, especially in the controversy between Georg Lukács, Johannes R. Becher, and Andor Gabor on the one side, and Bertolt Brecht, Walter Benjamin, Hanns Eisler, and Ernst Bloch on the other. The discussion during this period is recorded and reexamined in Helga Gallas' excellent book *Marxistische Literaturtheorie* (Neuwied: Luchterhand, 1971).

All protagonists accept the central concept according to which art (the discussion is practically confined to literature) is determined, in its "truth content" as well as in its forms, by the class situation of the author (of course not simply in terms of his personal position and consciousness but of the objective correspondence of his work to the material and ideological position of the class). The conclusion which emerges from this discussion is that at the historical stage where the position of

the proletariat alone renders possible insight into the totality of
the social process, and into the necessity and direction of radical change (i.e., into "the truth"), only a proletarian literature
can fulfill the progressive function of art and develop a revolutionary consciousness: indispensable weapon in the class struggle.

Can such a literature arise in the traditional forms of art,
or will it develop new forms and techniques? This is the case of
the controversy: while Lukács (and with him the then
"official" Communist line) insists on the validity of the (re-
vamped) tradition (especially the great realistic novel of the
19th century), Brecht demands radically different forms (such
as the "epic theater"), and Benjamin calls for the transition
from the art form itself to such new technical expressions as the
film: "large, closed forms versus small, open forms."

In a sense, the confrontation between closed and open
forms seems no longer an adequate expression of the problem:
compared with today's anti-art, Brecht's open forms appear as
"traditional" literature. The problem is rather the underlying
concept of a *proletarian world view* which, by virtue of its
(particular) class character, represents the truth which art
must communicate if it is to be authentic art. This theory

> presupposes the existence of a proletarian world view.
> But precisely this presupposition does not stand up to
> an even tentative (*annähernde*) examination.*

This is a statement of fact—and a theoretical insight. If
the term "proletarian world view" is to mean the world view
that is prevalent among the working class, then it is, in the advanced capitalist countries, a world view shared by a large part
of the other classes, especially the middle classes. (In ritual-

* Gallas, *loc. cit.*, p. 73.

ized Marxist language, it would be called petty bourgeois reformist consciousness.) If the term is to designate *revolutionary* consciousness (latent or actual), then it is today certainly
not distinctively or even predominantly "proletarian"—not
only because the revolution against global monopoly capitalism is more and other than a proletarian revolution, but
also because its conditions, prospects, and goals cannot be adequately formulated in terms of a proletarian revolution (see
Chapter 1). And if this revolution is to be (in whatever form)
present as a goal in literature, such literature could not be typically proletarian.

This is at least the conclusion suggested by Marxian
theory. I recall again the dialectic of the universal and the particular in the concept of the proletariat: as a class in but not of
capitalist society, its particular interest (its own liberation) is
at the same time the general interest: it cannot free itself without abolishing itself as a class, and all classes. This is not an
"ideal," but the very dynamic of the socialist revolution. It follows that the goals of the proletariat *as revolutionary class* are
self-transcendent: while remaining historical, concrete goals,
they extend, in their class content, beyond the specific class
content. And if such transcendence is an essential quality of all
art, it follows that the goals of the revolution may find expression in bourgeois art, and in all forms of art. It seems to be
more than a matter of personal preference if Marx had a conservative taste in art, and Trotsky as well as Lenin were critical
of the notion of a "proletarian culture." *

It is therefore no paradox, and no exception, when even
specifically proletarian contents find their home in "bourgeois
literature." They are often accompanied by a kind of linguistic
revolution, which replaces the language of the ruling class by
that of the proletariat—without exploding the traditional form
(of the novel, the drama). Or, conversely, the proletarian revo-

* Gallas, *loc. cit.*, pp. 210 f.

lutionary contents are formed in the "high," stylized language of (traditional) poetry: as in Brecht's *Three Penny Opera* and *Mahagonny* and in the "artistic" prose of his *Galilei*.

The spokesmen for a specifically proletarian literature tried to save this notion by establishing a sweeping criterion that would allow to reject the "reformist" bourgeois radicals, namely, the appearance, in the work, of the basic laws which govern capitalist society. Lukács himself made this the shibboleth by which to identify authentic revolutionary literature. But precisely this requirement offends the very nature of art. The basic structure and dynamic of society can never find sensuous, aesthetic expression: they are, in Marxian theory, the essence behind the appearance, which can only be attained through scientific analysis, and formulated only in the terms of such an analysis. The "open form" cannot close the gap between the scientific truth and its aesthetic appearance. The introduction, into the play or the novel, of montage, documentation, reportage may well (as in Brecht) become an essential part of the aesthetic form—but it can do so only as a subordinate part.

Art can indeed become a weapon in the class struggle by promoting changes in the prevailing consciousness. However, the cases where a transparent correlation exists between the respective *class* consciousness and the work of art are extremely rare (Molière, Beaumarchais, Defoe). By virtue of its own subversive quality, art is associated with revolutionary consciousness, but to the degree to which the prevailing consciousness of a class is affirmative, integrated, blunted, revolutionary art will be opposed to it. Where the proletariat is non-revolutionary, revolutionary literature will *not* be proletarian literature. Nor can it be "anchored" in the prevailing (non-revolutionary) consciousness: only the *rupture*, the *leap*, can prevent the resurrection of the "false" consciousness in a socialist society.

The fallacies which surround the notion of a revolutionary literature are still aggravated in today's cultural revolution. The anti-intellectualism rampant in the New Left champions the demand for a working class literature which expresses the worker's actual interests and "emotions." For example:

"Intellectual pundits of the Left" are blamed for their "revolutionary aesthetic," and a "certain coterie of talmudists" is taken to task for being more "expert in weighing the many shadings and nuances of a word than involvement in the revolutionary process." * Archaic anti-intellectualism abhors the idea that the former may be an essential part of the latter, part of that translation of the world into a new language which may communicate the radically new claims of liberation.

Such spokesmen for the proletarian ideology criticize the cultural revolution as a "middle class trip." The philistine mind is at its very best when it proclaims that this revolution will "become meaningful" only "when it begins to understand the very real cultural meaning that a washing machine, for instance, has for a working class family with small children in diapers." And the philistine mind demands that "the artists of that revolution . . . tune in on the emotions of that family on the day, after months of debate and planning, that the washing machine is delivered . . ." **

This demand is reactionary not only from an artistic but also from a political point of view. Regressive are, not the emotions of the working class family, but the idea to make them into a standard for authentic radical and socialist literature: what is proclaimed to be the focal point of a revolutionary new culture is in fact the adjustment to the established one.

To be sure, the cultural revolution must recognize and subvert this atmosphere of the working class home, but this will not be done by "tuning in" on the emotions aroused by the

* Irvin Silber, in *Guardian*, December 13, 1969.
** Irvin Silber, in *Guardian*, December 6, 1969, p. 17.

delivery of a washing machine. On the contrary, such empathy perpetuates the prevailing "atmosphere."

The concept of proletarian literature = revolutionary literature remains questionable even if it is freed from the "tuning in" on *prevailing* emotions, and, instead, related to the *most advanced* working class consciousness. This would be a political consciousness, and prevalent only among a minority of the working class. If art and literature would reflect such advanced consciousness, they would have to express the actual conditions of the class struggle and the actual prospects of subverting the capitalist system. But precisely these brutally political contents *militate* against their aesthetic transformation—therefore the very valid objection against "pure art." However, these contents also militate against a less pure translation into art, namely, the translation into the concreteness of the daily life and practice. Lukács has, on these grounds, criticized a representative workers' novel of the time: the personages of this novel talk at the dinner table at home the same language as a delegate at a party meeting.*

A revolutionary literature in which the working class is the subject-object, and which is the historical heir, the definite negation, of "bourgeois" literature, remains a thing of the future.

But what holds true for the notion of revolutionary art with respect to the working classes in the advanced capitalist countries does not apply to the situation of the racial minorities in these countries, and the majorities in the Third World. I have already referred to black music; there is also a black literature, especially poetry, which may well be called revolutionary: it lends voice to a total rebellion which finds expression in the aesthetic form. It is not a "class" literature, and its particular content is at the same time the universal one: what is at

* Gallas, *loc. cit.*, p. 121. A Communist participant in the discussion remarked correctly that, in this case, one should call things by their name and speak not of art or literature but of propaganda.

stake in the specific situation of the oppressed racial minority is the most general of all needs, namely, the very existence of the individual and his group as *human beings*. The most extreme political content does not repel traditional forms.

The common denominator for the misplaced radicalism in the cultural revolution is the anti-intellectualism which it shares with the most reactionary representatives of the Establishment: revolt against Reason—not only against the Reason of capitalism, bourgeois society, and so on, but against Reason *per se*. And just as the indeed urgent fight against the training of cadres for the Establishment *in* the universities turns into a fight against *the* university, so the destruction of the aesthetic form turns into a destruction of art. To be sure, in both branches of the intellectual culture, isolation and alienation from the given reality may indeed lead to an "ivory tower," but may also (and do) lead to something that the Establishment is increasingly incapable of tolerating, namely, independent thinking and feeling.

4

CONCLUSION

But with all its misplaced radicalism, the movement is still the most advanced counterforce. It has extended the rebellion to two main thrusts: it has drawn into the political struggle the realm of nonmaterial needs (of self-determination, nonalienated human relationships), and the physiological dimension of existence: the realm of nature. The emancipation of sensibility is the common ground. It engenders a new experience of a world violated by the requirements of the established society, and of the vital need for total transformation. What has become intolerable is the overwhelming unity of opposites in this world: unity of pleasure and horror, calm and violence, gratification and destruction, beauty and ugliness, which hits us tangibly in our daily life environment. The prevailing contempt for "aesthetic snobbism" should no longer deter us from articulating this experience: the repulsive unity of opposites (most

129

concrete and unsublimated manifestation of capitalist dialectic!) has become the life element of the system; the protest
against these conditions must become a political weapon.

The fight will be won when the obscene symbiosis of opposites is broken—the symbiosis between the erotic play of the
sea (its waves rolling in as advancing males, breaking by their
own grace, turning female: caressing each other, and licking
the rocks) and the booming death industries at its shores, between the flight of the white birds and that of the gray air
force jets, between the silence of the night and the vicious farts
of the motorcycles . . . Only then will men and women be free
to resolve the conflict between the Fifth Avenues and the ghettos, between procreation and genocide. In the long range, the
political dimension can no longer be divorced from the aesthetic, reason from sensibility, the gesture of the barricade
from that of love. To be sure, the former spells hatred—but the
hatred of all that which is inhuman, and this "gut hatred" is an
essential ingredient of the cultural revolution.

It is utterly unpopular; the people hate it, "the masses" de-
spise it. Perhaps they feel that the rebellion really strikes out
against the whole, against all its rotten taboos—that it endan-
gers the necessity, the value, of their performance, their fun,
the prosperity around them. Prevailing is the resentment
against the new morality, the feminine gesture, the contempt
for the jobs of the Establishment—resentment against the rebels who permit themselves what the people have to forgo and
repress.

Wilhelm Reich was right in emphasizing the roots of fascism in instinctual repression; he was wrong when he saw the
mainsprings for the defeat of fascism in sexual liberation. The
latter can proceed quite far without endangering the capitalist
system at the advanced stage (where the quantity of physical
human labor power and the working day are progressively reducible). Beyond this stage, instinctual liberation becomes a

force of social liberation only to the degree to which sexual energy is transformed into erotic energy, striving to change the mode of life on a social, political scale. Today at least, submissiveness, aggression, and the identification of the people with their leaders have a rational rather than an instinctual basis: the leaders still deliver the goods (and, periodically, the bodies of the enemies who threaten the continued delivery of these goods). This is the basis on which the hatred and aggression against the rebels are articulated and organized. And the instinctual rebellion will have become a political force only when it is accompanied and guided by the rebellion of reason: the absolute refusal of the intellect (and the intelligentsia) to lend their support to the Establishment, and the mobilization of the power of theoretical and practical reason for the work of change.

The fetishism of the commodity world, which seems to become denser every day, can be destroyed only by men and women who have torn aside the technological and ideological veil which conceals what is going on, which covers the insane rationality of the whole—men and women who have become free to develop their own needs, to build, in solidarity, their own world. The end of reification is the beginning of the individual: the new Subject of radical reconstruction. And the genesis of this Subject is a process which shatters the traditional framework of radical theory and practice. The ideas and goals of the cultural revolution have their foundation in the actual historical situation. They have a chance of becoming truly concrete, of affecting the whole if the rebels succeed in subjecting the new sensibility (the private, individual liberation) to the rigorous discipline of the mind (*die Anstrengung des Begriffs*). The latter alone can protect the movement from the entertainment industry and the nut house, by channeling its energies into socially relevant manifestations. And the more the insane power of the whole seems to justify any spontaneous counteraction (no matter how self-destructive), the more must despair and defiance be subjected to political discipline and *organization*. The revolution is nothing without its own rationality. The liberating laughter of the Yippies, their radical inability to take the bloody game of "justice," of "law and order," seriously, may help to tear the ideological veil but leaves intact the structure behind the veil. The latter can be brought down only by those who still sustain the established work process, who constitute its human base, who reproduce its profits and its power. They include an ever-increasing sector of the middle classes, and of the intelligentsia. At present, only a small part of this huge, truly underlying population is moving and is aware. To help extend this movement and this awareness is the constant task of the still isolated radical groups.

To prepare the ground for this development makes the emancipation of *consciousness* still the primary task. Without it, all emancipation of the senses, all radical activism, remains blind, self-defeating. Political practice still depends on theory (only the Establishment can dispense with it!): on education, persuasion—on Reason.

There is one argument against this "intellectualism" which must still be discussed. The gist of the argument is this: The emphasis on theory and education diverts mental and physical energy from the arena in which the struggle against the existing society will be decided—the political arena. It transfigures economic and social into cultural conditions; it is absorbed in abstract intellectual problems while brutal force is about to exterminate the desperate resistance movements the world over. Thus, behind the weighty title of "cultural revolution" (borrowed from a country where it is a mass movement) is nothing but a private, particular, ideological revolt: an insult to the suffering masses.

The slogan "let's sit down and reason together" has rightly become a joke. Can you reason with the Pentagon on any other thing than the relative effectiveness of killing machines—and their price? The Secretary of State can reason with the Secretary of the Treasury, and the latter with another Secretary and his advisers, and they all can reason with Members of the Board of the great corporations. This is incestuous reasoning; they are all in agreement about the basic issue: the strengthening of the established power structure. Reasoning "from without" the power structure is a naïve idea. They will listen only to the extent to which the voices can be translated into votes, which may perhaps bring into office another set of the same power structure with the same ultimate concern.

The argument is overwhelming. Bertolt Brecht noted that we live at a time where it seems a crime to talk about a tree. Since then, things have become much worse. Today, it seems a crime merely to *talk* about change while one's society is transformed into an institution of violence, terminating in Asia the genocide which began with the liquidation of the American Indians. Is not the sheer power of this brutality immune against the spoken and written word which indicts it? And is not the word which is directed against the practitioners of this power the same they use to defend their power? There is a level on which even the unintelligent action against them seems justified. For action smashes, though only for a moment, the closed universe of suppression. Escalation is built into the system and accelerates the counterrevolution unless it is stopped in time.

And yet, there is a time for talk and a time for action also in this system, and these times are defined (marked) by the concrete social constellation of forces. Where radical mass action is absent, and the Left is incomparably weaker, its actions must be self-limiting. What is imposed on the rebellion by intensified repression and the concentration of destructive forces in the hands of the power structure must become the soil for regrouping, reexamination. Strategies must be developed which are adapted to combat the counterrevolution. The outcome depends, to a great extent, on the ability of the young generation—not to drop out and not to accommodate, but to learn how to regroup after defeat, how to develop, with the new sensibility a new rationality, to sustain the long process of education—the indispensable prerequisite for the transition to large-scale political action. For the next revolution will be the concern of generations, and "the final crisis of capitalism" may take all but a century.

LIST OF WORKS CITED

Adorno, Theodor W., *Aesthetische Theorie* (Frankfurt/Main: Suhrkamp, 1970).

Adorno, Theodor W., Else Frenkel-Brunswik, and others, *The Authoritarian Personality* (New York: Harper and Brothers, 1950).

Aronowitz, Stanley, "Does the United States Have a New Working Class?" in *The Revival of American Socialism,* edited by George Fisher (New York: Oxford University Press, 1971).

Artaud, Antonin, *Le Théâtre et son double* (Paris: Gallimard, 1964).

Baran, Paul A., and Paul M. Sweezy, *Monopoly Capitalism* (New York: Monthly Review Press, 1966).

Basso, Lelio, *Zur Theorie des politischen Konflicts* (Frankfurt: Suhrkamp, 1969).

Berger, John, *The Moment of Cubism* (New York: Pantheon, 1969).

Bookchin, Murray, "Ecology and Revolutionary Thought" and "Towards a Liberatory Technology," in *Post-Scarcity Anarchism* (Berkeley: Ramparts Press, 1971).

Breton, André, *Manifestos of Surrealism,* translation by R. Scaver and Helen R. Lane (Ann Arbor: University of Michigan Press, 1969).

135

Budish, J. M., *The Changing Structure of the Working Class* (New York: International Publishers, 1964).

Calvert, Greg, and Carol Neiman, *A Disrupted History: The New Left and the New Capitalism* (New York: Random House, 1971).

Domhoff, G. William, *Who Rules America?* (Englewood Cliffs: Prentice-Hall, 1967).

Fernier, Robert, *Gustave Courbet* (Paris: Bibliothèque des Arts, 1969), quotation by André Fernigier.

Fry, Edward, *On the Future of Art*, essays by Arnold J. Toynbee, Louis I. Kahn, and others (New York: Viking Press, 1970).

Gallas, Helga, *Marxistische Literaturtheorie* (Neuwied: Luchterhand, 1971).

Gillman, Joseph M., *Prosperity in Crisis* (New York: Marzani and Munsell, 1965).

Gintis, Herbert, "The New Working Class and Revolutionary Youth," in *Socialist Revolution*, San Francisco, May–June 1970.

Gorz, André, "Technique, Techniciens et Lutte des Classes," in *Les Temps Modernes*, August–September 1971.

Hegel, G. W. F., *Vorlesugen über die Aesthetik* (*Sämmtliche Werke*), edited by Glockner (Stuttgart: Frommann, 1928), vol. XIII; translation by F. P. R. Osmaston, *The Philosophy of Fine Art* (London: G. Bell and Sons, 1920), vol. II.

Julien, Claude, *L'Empire américain* (Paris: Grasset, 1968).

Kolko, Gabriel, *Wealth and Power in America* (New York: Praeger, 1962).

Lowenfeld, Henry and Yela, "Our Permissive Society and the Superego," in *The Psychoanalytic Quarterly*, October 1970.

Lowenthal, Leo, *Literature and the Image of Man* (Boston: Beacon Press, 1957).

Lowenthal, Leo, and Norbert Guterman, *Prophets of Deceit:*

A Study of the Techniques of the American Agitator, 1949 (Palo Alto: Pacific Books, 1970).

Luxemburg, Rosa, *Politische Schriften,* edited by O. Flechtheim (Frankfurt: Europäische Verlagsanstalt, 1968).

Magdoff, Harry, *The Age of Imperialism* (New York: Monthly Review Press, 1970).

Magri, Lucio, "Parlement ou Conseils" (1970) in *Il Manifesto: Analyses et Theses* . . . , edited by Rossana Rossanda (Paris: Editions du Seuil, 1971).

Mandel, Ernest, *La Réponse socialiste au défi américain* (Paris: Maspero, 1969).

Mandel, Ernest, "Workers and Permanent Revolution," in *The Revival of American Socialism,* edited by George Fisher (New York: Oxford University Press, 1971).

Il Manifesto: Theses, in *Politics and Society,* vol. 1, no. 4, August 1971.

Marcuse, Herbert, *Eros and Civilization* (Boston: Beacon Press, 1955, 1966).

Marcuse, Herbert, *An Essay on Liberation* (Boston: Beacon Press, 1969).

Marcuse, Herbert, *Negations* (Boston, Beacon Press: 1968).

Marx, Karl, *Capital* (New York: Modern Library).

Marx, Karl, *The Economic and Philosophic Manuscripts of 1844,* edited by Dirk J. Struik (New York: International Publishers, 1964).

Marx, Karl, *Grundrisse der Kritik der Politischen Oekonomie* (Berlin: Dietz, 1953).

Marx, Karl, *Resultate des unmittelbaren Produktionprozesses* (earlier version of a sixth chapter of *Capital*) (Frankfurt/Main: Neue Kritik, 1969).

Melman, Seymour, *Pentagon Capitalism* (New York: McGraw-Hill, 1970).

Merleau-Ponty, Maurice, *La Prose du monde* (Paris: Gallimard, 1969).

Merleau-Ponty, Maurice, *Sens et Non-Sens* (Paris: Nagel, 1948).

Morawski, Stefan, "Artistic Value," in *The Journal of Aesthetic Education,* vol. 5, no. 1.

Paradise Now, Collective Creation of the Living Theatre, written down by Judith Melina and Julian Beck (New York: Random House, 1971).

The Pentagon Papers—The Senator Gravel Edition, 4 vols. (Boston: Beacon Press, 1971).

Raphael, Max, *The Demands of Art,* translation by Norbert Guterman, Bolingen Series, LXXVII (Princeton: Princeton University Press, 1968).

Read, Herbert, ed., *Surrealism,* with an introduction by the editor (New York: Harcourt, Brace and Co., 1936).

Schmidt, Alfred, *Der Begriff der Natur in der Lehre von Marx* (Frankfurt: Europäische Verlagsanstalt, 1962).

Schnapp, Alain, and Pierre Vidal-Naquet, eds., *Journal de la Commune Etudiante, Novembre 1967–Juin 1968:* Textes et Documents (Paris: Editions du Seuil, 1968; abridged American edition, *The French Student Uprising, November 1967–June 1968,* translated by Maria Jolas (Boston: Beacon Press, 1971).

Schopenhauer, Arthur, *The World As Will and Representation,* translated by E. F. J. Payne (New York: Dover).

Tanzer, Michael, *The Sick Society* (New York: Holt, Rinehart and Winston, 1971).

Teodori, Massimo, ed., *The New Left: A Documentary History* (New York: Bobbs-Merrill, 1969).

Zeitlin, Maurice, ed., *American Society, Inc.* (Chicago: Markham, 1970).